SAINT PETERSBURG

PETERHOF · TSARSKOYE SELO · PAVLOVSK · GATCHINA · ORANIENBAUM · KRONSTADT

SAINT PETERSBURG

PETERHOF
TSARSKOYE SELO
PAVLOVSK
GATCHINA
ORANIENBAUM
KRONSTADT

ИВАН ФЕДОРОВ

Text

Natalia Popova
and Andrei Fedorov

Translation

Gillian Kenyon

Design

Nikolai Kutovoy
Evgueny Kutovoy

Photographs

Serguei Alexeev
Vladimir Antoshchenkov
Valentin Baranovsky
Nikolai Berketov
Leonid Bogdanov
Sergei Chistobaev
Vladimir Davydov
Pavel Demidov
Vladimir Denisov
Konstantin Doka
Natalia Doka
Vladimir Filippov
Alexander Fomichev
Leonid Gerkus
Eduard Gorbatenko
Alexander Gronsky
Alexander Kashnitsky
Leonard Kheifets
Artur Kirakozov
Pavel Kuzmichev
Mikhail Manin
Vladimir Melnikov
Yury Molodkovets
Nikolai Rakhmanov
Alexander Riazantsev
Viktor Savik
Georgy Shablovsky
Nikolai Shalyakin
Vladimir Shlakan
Evgueny Shlepkin
Evgueny Siniaver
Vladimir Terebenin
Oleg Trubsky
Vasily Vorontsov
Leonid Yakutin
Kira Zharinova

Editors

Irina Kharitonova
Irina Lvova

Computer layout

Elena Morozova

Colour correction

Viacheslav Bykovski
Ekaterina Fomenko
Vladimir Glaskov
Vladimir Kniazev
Alexander Kondratov
Liubov Kornilova
Denis Lazarev
Serguei Ludzski
Alexander Miagkov
Dmitry Trofimov
Serguei Vyrtosu

ISBN 5-8194-0041-0

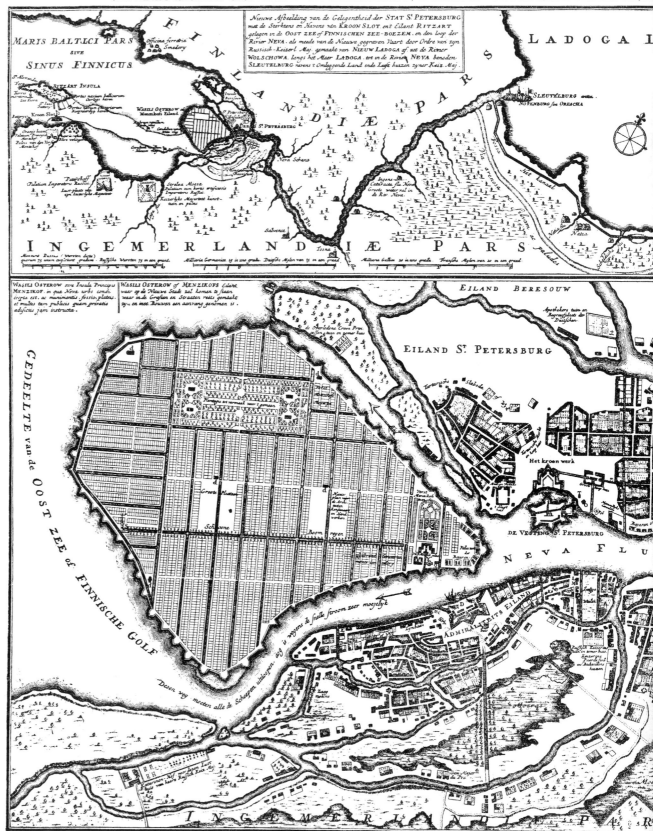

Benoit Coffre. 1671–1722
Portrait of Peter the Great

The city of St Petersburg, the former capital of the Russian Empire and the embodiment of the pride and glory of the Russian state, was founded on 27 May 1703.

The creation of the city was a daring feat. In order to realise his vision, Peter I, turning his back on the traditions of "ancient" Rus, called upon the new generation, which, with its fierce confidence and characteristic youthfulness, welcomed his ambitious plans. St Petersburg became the symbol of a new era of Russian history and grandiose, unprecedented ventures. As if challenging nature itself, the Emperor resolved to create a northern "Paradise" on an area of marshy land that seemed perpetually wreathed in mist. Petersburg became the primary concern and favourite "child of the northern giant, in which the energy, brutality and revolutionary force of the '93 Convention were concentrated,...[the favourite child] of the tsar, who renounced his country for its own good and oppressed it in the name of Europeanism and civilisation" (Alexander Herzen). Indeed, the building of the new capital demanded a concerted effort and a great deal of strength. Many thousands of human lives were lost in the process, and it is perhaps because of this that the history of Petersburg is so full of dark and tragic events. During the three hundred years of its existence, it has endured more than its fair share of historical and natural disasters.

In times of war, hostile forces have tried again and again to capture the city, thinking to erase it from the face of the earth, but not once has an army succeeded in setting foot within its limits. Even the most terrifying blockade in the history of mankind, lasting 872 days from 8 September 1941 to 27 January 1944, was unable to break the spirit of the city's inhabitants.

In the autumn, the merciless elements threaten to wreak havoc on the long, flat banks of the River Neva. Three terrible deluges, which have occurred with an alarming regularity every hundred years (1724, 1824 and 1924), and other less significant

floods have sought to destroy this manmade wonder, yet the city has stood its ground.

The unpredictability of the elements makes Petersburg a profoundly expressive city. It has the ability to change its countenance unexpectedly, compelling us to see its beauty in a new light. It is as if the city senses the mood of its inhabitants and seeks to share with them both their joy and melancholy. The most enchanting time, however, is that of the famous White Nights, which last from mid-May to mid-July, when the city casts its spell over locals and visitors alike. These few months seem almost to compensate for the frequent rains, clammy mists, short winter days and long autumn nights. "A multitude of poets have extolled and described our northern nights, but to express their beauty in words is as impossible as describing the scent of a rose and the tremor of a string fading into air. No poet can convey the inexpressible, mysterious silence, pregnant with thoughts and life, that rests on the heavily respiring Neva after the heat of day in the phosphorescent light of the frail clouds and crimson west. No painter can capture the wondrous shades and hues that play in the sky and are reflected in the rivers as on the skin of a chameleon, in the facets of crystal or the polarisation of light. No musician can transpose into earthly tongues the sounds, permeated with feeling, that rise up from the earth to the skies only to fall back to earth once more reflected by the heavens" (Apollon Grigoriev).

St Petersburg is the "strangest of all Russian cities." It is a unique entity with a highly pronounced individuality and a complex and subtle spirit, which leads a mysterious, dramatic life of its own. No other Russian city is the subject of so many myths and legends. No other city has aroused such mixed responses from the very moment it was born: it has been loved and hated, lauded and damned, but it has left no one indifferent. "What a city! What a river! An unparalleled city! One must part

with Petersburg for a short time and see the old capitals, ramshackle Paris and sooty London, in order to appreciate Petersburg's worth. Look what harmony! How all the parts complement the whole! Such beautiful buildings, such taste and altogether such variety springing from the union of water and buildings." Dating from the early 19th century, these are the words of the famous Russian poet Konstantin Batiushkov, a man with a keen sense of the beauty of Petersburg.

The reason why this most "contrived" city was so remarkable was that "its appearance bears the mark of a deliberate human creation." It began with thoughts and ideas laid out in a plan. The open stretches of dry land and the lines of the Neva and the canals became formative elements in the design of Petersburg. Here, emphasis was placed less on erecting individual buildings than on creating entire artificial panoramas. Architects were careful to contrive long vistas. The idiosyncrasies of the design of the northern capital can be seen clearly from a bird's eye view. "Everything appears flat, the city's unevenness is erased, and before us lies a faintly outlined relief, like a plan. Yet the observer is able to see the city within the framework of nature. It is as if nature is closing in on the city, while the city casts its reflection on the surrounding landscape" (Nikolai Antsiferov).

Petersburg also owes its uniqueness to its geographical location: it stands on the edge of the vast territory of Russia and is indeed a "window onto Europe". From the west it has not only been buffeted by the waters of the autumn floods, but also by the shocks of historic disasters endured by the West. European ideas and the joys and woes of the "old continent" have been borne in on the Baltic winds.

St Petersburg threw its doors open wide to everyone who accepted the invitation to take part in the ambitious and rather risky business of its creation. The young city was notable for its receptivity to the cultural achievements of Europe and

the knowledge and skills of its foreign guests. In other countries, schools were established first, followed by universities, and only once a significant number of scholars had emerged were academies founded. In Peter's day, the first schools were only beginning to take shape in Russia and not a single university existed, yet the tsar-reformer had already decided to invite learned foreigners (mainly from Germany) to Petersburg to create an Academy of Sciences. He offered them the opportunity to conduct scientific research at the expense of the state in return for introducing young Russian men to the principles of science.

Artists, architects, sculptors and engravers were also invited to Russia to sow the seeds of the European fine arts in the damp soil on the banks of the Neva. Petersburg swiftly absorbed and assimilated all things beautiful. Germans, Swedes, Italians, Dutch-, French- and Englishmen initially made their homes in separate colonies, but the national and linguistic boundaries gradually disappeared. Within a short time, a unique nation had arisen – the nation of Petersburg, in which locals and Russified foreigners lived in harmony.

For many who came to Petersburg, the city became a second home to which they devoted their energy and talents. Together with Russian experts, they worked to create a city and build splendid country residences for the ruling elite. Some people believe that "Petersburg doesn't have an ounce of originality: it is simply a kind of general embodiment of the notion of a capital city, and is the spit and image of any other major city in the world" (Vissarion Belinsky). Yet nothing could be further from the truth. European architectural forms metamorphosed under the influences of Russian architecture, resulting in the emergence of genuinely unique edifices. In art, as in the social and everyday life of the city, European and Russian traditions merged to create an entirely new phenomenon – the culture of St Petersburg.

Vasily Sadovnikov
Panorama of the Nevsky Prospekt. 1830–1835. Lithograph

SAINT

PETERSBURG

For the first few years, construction work was centred on the Hare Island. Here, the fortress of Sankt Pieter Burkh was erected as the nucleus of the future city. Its location was selected by Peter the Great himself who well understood the strategic advantages of placing such an outpost on the island in the Neva delta. Within a year, six bastions (the projecting portions of a fortification) had been raised. Although the bastions were made of earth (substituted with stone in 1740), building the new city out of stone was one of Peter's greatest concerns. A special decree was issued prohibiting the construction of stone edifices elsewhere in Russia, and all the master stonemasons were ordered to the banks of the Neva. Peter also introduced an unusual "stone toll": every boat and every string of carts to enter the city had to bring a certain number of stones with it.

The fortress was designed as a closed rampart consisting of bastions and curtains (the part of the wall connecting the bastions). Peter was in a hurry to complete the job before the winter and so the construction of the fortifications was carried out under the supervision of the tsar's closest associates, thus the bastions are named in honour of these men, to wit, Naryshkin, Trubetskoy, Zotov, Golovkin and Menshikov. One of the southern bastions was built under the direct observation of Peter himself and consequently became known as the Tsar Bastion. On the eastern side of the island, in the curtain that links the Tsar Bastion with the Menshikov Bastion, the main gates to the fortress – St Peter's Gate – were installed. They were protected by a ravelin (a V-shaped outwork incorporated into the design of the ramparts), which was named in honour of Saint John. In order to get into the fortress it was necessary to cross the wooden St John's Bridge, pass through St John's Gate and then through a second gateway – St Peter's Gate (built in stone to replace the original wooden structure in 1714–1718, architect: Domenico Trezzini). The triumphal arch of the latter still bears a beautifully preserved double-headed eagle (the coat-of-arms of the Russian Empire) wearing

THE PETER AND PAUL
FORTRESS

1 White Nights. Peter and Paul
Fortress seen from the Trinity Bridge

12

The Peter and Paul Fortress
never served a direct military
purpose, since no enemy ever
made it as far as its walls.
Very soon after it had been built,
however, it began to be used
as a political prison and torture-
chamber. Over the course of two
hundred years, its bastions
and casemates held countless
enemies of the state.
To the southwest of the cathedral
a ravelin was constructed, which
was later named in honour of
Tsarevich Alexei. It is to this place
above all that the infamy of the
Peter and Paul Fortress is linked.
In February 1718, Peter I
brought his own son, Alexei, here
together with a number of other
conspirators. After enduring
horrific tortures, conducted, so
historians claim, in the presence
of the Emperor himself, Alexei
was killed. The Supreme Court
that passed the death sentence
consisted of 127 people. Only
one of them, B.P. Sheremetev,
refused to sign the ruling.
Throughout the 18th century,
many people experienced the
horrors of the fortress's casemates. Amongst them was the
not unknown adventuress who
aspired to the Russian throne,
passing herself off as Princess
Tarakanova, the alleged secret
daughter of Elizabeth Petrovna.
Empress Catherine II entrusted
Count Alexei Orlov with
a secret mission to bring the
pretender to Petersburg.

2 View from the belfry
of the Sts Peter and Paul Cathedral

3 View of St John's Gate

4 St Peter's Gate. 1714–1718,
architect: Domenico Trezzini
sculptors: Hans Konrad Osner,
Nicolas Pinod

The latter lived in Livorno, for which the count at once set sail. Orlov was a fine figure of a man with a solid physique and a powerful air of courage and magnanimity. Catherine herself compared him to "the heroes of Ancient Rome". Having seduced the young woman, the count tricked her onto the ship that was to bring Tarakanova to Russia. On the night of 24 May 1775, she was imprisoned in the fortress. After being tortured and racked with consumption, she finally died on 4 December 1775. The famous Petersburg historian and area studies specialist, Mikhail Pyliaev wrote: "Legend has it that towards the end of his life the count was tormented by melancholy and at night he saw visions of the unhappy woman whom he had seduced. The story goes that after Tarakanova had been brought from overseas, the count was received very graciously by the Empress, yet with a noticeable coldness; Her Majesty, as a woman, could not properly appreciate the doings of the ambitious man who had betrayed a woman who loved him and commanded feelings of love out of cold calculation."
The real Princess Tarakanova died in 1810 under the name of Sister Dosiphea in St John's Convent outside Moscow. After a meeting with Catherine, she herself chose such a fate.

5 Domes and belfry
of the Sts Peter and Paul Cathedral

6 Entrance to the Peter
and Paul Fortress

imperial crowns, made of lead and weighing over a tonne. Beyond St Peter's Gate the path is lined by two squat military buildings: to the right is the Artillery Arsenal (1801), and to the left is the Engineer's House (1749). By 1787, the entire fortress was clad in granite. A signal tower and flagpole for a special fortress standard, were installed on the Naryshkin Bastion, which also became the site of a cannon, fired every day at noon, a tradition that has been preserved to this day.

The main building within the fortress is the Sts Peter and Paul Cathedral (1712–1733, architect: Domenico Trezzini). Its shape is somewhat reminiscent of that of an 18th century ship: the high eastern wall is the stern, while the tall spire is the mast. The design of the church, including the decorative fittings inside, is indicative of the typical Petersburg practice of combining the traditions of western religious architecture and Ancient Russian church design. Thus, the interior of the cathedral includes both a carved wooden iconostasis executed after the Orthodox traditions, and a carved pulpit for the preacher, as in a Catholic church. Unusual too for an Orthodox religious building are the tower clocks on the belfry with their chiming bells.

This belfry together with the gilded spire and figure of an angel, the guardian of the city, stands at a height of 122.5 metres. At the time it was the tallest building in Russia. The figure of the angel serves as a weather vane, indicating the direction of the wind. Stretching boldly towards the heavens, the cathedral spire became an integral part of the Petersburg skyline from the moment it first appeared. The interior of the cathedral is designed like a ceremonial hall, divided by piers into three naves. Its main feature is the carved gilded iconostasis (1722–1729, designed by the architects Domenico Trezzini and Ivan Zarudny). The central section of the iconostasis resembles a triumphal arch, a symbolic celebration of the glorious victory of the Russian troops in the Northern War. The lavishness and grandeur of the architectural forms of this altar screen combined with countless sculptures creates the kind of stunning decorative effect that is typical of the Baroque style.

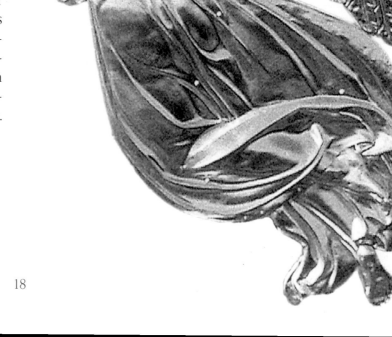

7 Angel on top of the Peter
and Paul Cathedral

8 Peter and Paul Fortress. View of Cathedral Square
Sts Peter and Paul Cathedral. 1712–1733, architect: Domenico Trezzini
Boat House. 1762–1765, architect: Alexander Vist

Beyond the *tsarskie vrata* (*the royal gates* or central doors in the iconostasis) there is a richly decorated canopy over the table used in the performance of religious ceremonies. It was fashioned after Lorenzo Bernini's canopy in St Peter's Cathedral in Rome.

In the 1830s, in the right-hand row of piers, the *imperial (tsar's) place* was installed, made up of a small dais under a carved wooden canopy where the Emperor or Empress would stand during services. The canopy is decorated with drapes of raspberry velvet and its carved peak is crowned with the representation of a pillow bearing the royal regalia. Opposite the *tsar's place* is the pulpit, decorated with wooden statues of the Apostles Peter and Paul, the four Evangelists and the Holy Spirit in the form of a dove surrounded by clouds and cherubim. The pulpit is additionally decorated with paintings on Gospel subjects. This splendid example of Russian woodcarving was installed here in 1732.

9 Sts Peter and Paul Cathedral
Pulpit

10 Sts Peter and Paul Cathedral
Tsar's place

11 Sts Peter and Paul Cathedral
Interior

ЦРЦА ВЕРСА́ВИА

КНЗЬ
АЛЕⰌАНДРЪ НЕВⰌКИ

ЦРⰦЧЪ
ДИМИТРІⰦ

The Sts Peter and Paul Cathedral contains a significant
collection of paintings from
the Petrine era. The face
of the iconostasis incorporates
43 icons, set out somewhat
differently to those in the Russian
Orthodox1 churches. The right
section of the iconostasis,
the "male" section, includes
17 icons, 13 of which depict
Biblical characters. On the left
is the "female" section, showing
images of holy women.

12 Sts Peter and Paul Cathedral
Iconostasis. 1722–1729, designed
by Ivan Zarudny

13–17 Sts Peter and Paul Cathedral
Iconostasis. Icons: *Queen Bathsheba,
Holy Prince Alexander Nevsky,
Holy Prince Dimitry, Holy Prince
Vladimir, Holy Tsar Konstantin*
Mid-18th century, artists:
Alexei Protopopov, Andrei Pospelov

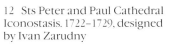

КНⰌ·ВЛАДИМІРЪ

ЦРЬ КОНСТАНТИНЪ

Amongst the Old Testament protagonists depicted on the icons are characters who have not been canonised by the Orthodox Church. These are the judge, Samson, bearing the gates of the city on his shoulders, the courageous Jael, who killed Sisera, the enemy of the Israelites, and the beautiful Bathsheba. The royal gates themselves are unusual – four panels covered with depictions of the Last Supper in bas-relief, and not a single icon in sight.

The cathedral is the imperial burial-vault. The tomb of Peter the Great is marked with the standards of the regiments which, under his leadership, conquered the Swedes in the Northern War (1700–1721). All of the Emperors and Grand Dukes lie under identical white marble sarcophagi, save for Alexander II and his wife Maria Alexandrovna, who was born a princess of Hessen-Darmstadt. Their graves are marked by sarcophagi made of coloured jasper by the workers of a mineral plant in the Urals as a sign of their gratitude for the abolition of serfdom.

In 1998, the remains of the last Russian Emperor, Nicholas II, and the various members of his family who were shot to death in Ekaterinburg in June 1918, were buried in the cathedral.

In the 19th century, the chambers in the bastions and the Secret House of the Alexeevsky Ravelin built in the reign of Paul I were never empty. In April 1849, for example, a large number of men who had been arrested in connection with the case of Butashevich-Petrashevsky were brought here, including the twenty-eight year old Dostoevsky. He was considered one of the most dangerous criminals amongst the Petrashevsky Circle. On 22 December 1849, Dostoevsky and twenty of his associates were to be shot on Semenovsky Square, but their sentence was changed at the last minute to hard labour.

18 Sts Peter and Paul Cathedral. Tombs of Peter the Great, Catherine I and Elizabeth Petrovna. 1865: architect Auguste Poirot

19 Sts Peter and Paul Cathedral. Tombs of Alexander II and Maria Alexandrovna. 1906 Designed by the architect Andrei Gun

20 Emperor Nicholas II Photograph

21 Empress Alexandra Fedorovna. Photograph

22 Sts Peter and Paul Cathedral. St Catherine Side-chapel. Grave of the last Emperor, Nicholas II, his wife, Alexandra Fedorovna, their children and members of the household

23 Nicholas II's children Photograph

25

Dostoevsky's wife, Anna Snitkina, recreated these terrifying moments of his life in her memoirs from his own words, describing how oppressed he had been by the thought of all the things he had not yet succeeded in doing or writing. The writer's reaction to the change in his sentence is understandable; when he was once again installed in a gloomy prison cell, having escaped death, he ...began to pace about merrily, humming to himself. One of the many places of incarceration that existed at different times within the fortress was the prison in the Trubetskoy Bastion (1708–1714). Those who died in solitary confinement within its walls, plagued by the stench and the damp, heard the melodious chimes of the Sts Peter and Paul Cathedral before they died. The last prisoners to be held in the Trubetskoy Bastion, from 1917–1919, were the ministers of the Provisional Government and the Grand Dukes. They were all shot in the Sts Peter and Paul Cathedral during the time of the "red terror". The prison in the Trubetskoy Bastion has since been turned into a museum.

Not far from the Sts Peter and Paul Cathedral is the Commandant's House (1743–1746) in which the commanding officer of the fortress lived. Over the course of two hundred years there were 32 commandants. It was an honoured position and was often held for life. It was awarded to generals of great merit who had earned the particular trust of the sovereign.

In one of the rooms of the Commandant's House, now the Memorial Hall, the Supreme Criminal Court would convene to hear the cases of the many political prisoners held in the Peter and Paul Fortress. Thus, on 12 July 1826, five Decembrists – Ryleev, Pestel, Muravev-Apostol, Bestuzhev-Riumin and Kakhovsky – were sentenced to death. These men had been responsible for the first protest

for freedom, the Constitution
and human rights in Russia.
The remaining participants
in the uprising, many of whom
were members of the nobility,
were sentenced to hard labour
in Siberia. Today, the Commandant's House contains
an exhibition about the history
of the city.
In 1992, a statue of Peter I,
the work of Mikhail Shemiakin,
was erected on the square in
front of the guardhouse and
soon became the subject of great
debate. This unusual image
is quite different to the typical
representations of the tsar-
creator and tsar-victor that
prevailed in the monumental
sculptures of centuries gone by.
Yet the longer the statue "lives"
in the fortress, the more normal
its presence becomes. Peter
calmly observes the inquisitive
tourists, poses for their cameras
and pays no attention to the
children who today know
no fear of the "bronze shadow"
of the formidable Emperor.

24 Commandant's House
1743–1746, architect:
Domenico Trezzini;
engineer: Jean de Marin

25 Commandant's House
Memorial Hall

26 Statue of Peter I, 1992,
sculptor: Mikhail Shemiakin

Petersburg is at once united and divided by the Neva. In May, the ice flows from the Lake Ladoga in the east drift past the columned facades of the city's palaces, bringing a cold northeastern wind with them. Since the time of Peter the Great, the Neva has been linked to the basin of the mighty Volga by a system of waterways. It is as if the cares of the vast territory of Russia, reaching right back to the Pacific, are carried along with the drifting ice and the winds from the east. Downstream from the Lieutenant Schmidt Bridge, freight ships, tankers and tourist liners from far and wide line the banks of Vasilievsky Island and the English Embankment. Occasionally, one of the few large sailboats that are still in use will winter here. Floating restaurants in the guise of old vessels can be seen on the Neva all year round, however. On very rare occasions, when Petersburg happens to be one of the finishing points of the international Cutty Sark Tall Ships' Races, the river becomes crowded with sailboats and the facades of the elegant residences lining the banks are obscured by a forest of masts and rigging. If the Neva is the city's main thoroughfare, then the Fontanka, the Moika and the numerous canals and channels are its streets and alleyways. During the day, the Neva is deserted. The "river trams" that once carried passengers around the centre of the city are no more. Freight transportation within the city limits has almost ceased, smoky long boats no longer moor along the embankments, and the lumbering barges that once

27 Peter and Paul Fortress
Neva Gate. 1784–1787,
architect: Nikolai Lvov

travelled the lengths of the Neva
have given way to motorboats
of various sizes scurrying to and
fro along the Nevka, the Fontanka and the Moika with cargoes
of sightseers.

During Peter's reign, there were
no bridges over the Neva.
The Emperor wanted the people
of Petersburg, to their dismay,
to share his passion for sailing,
thus riverboats were the common form of transport. Peter
even made it a tradition to take
his retinue out in rowing- and
sailing boats. Many members
of his circle set out on these
excursions praying to holy icons
in dread of the perfidious waters.
It was not until after the death
of the autocrat and "sailor" that
three floating bridges appeared
across the Neva. These were
dismantled at the time of the
spring thaws and the late
autumn freezes. Only in the mid-
19th century were they finally
replaced with permanent
bridges made of metal.

28 Spit of Vasilievsky Island
and the Peter and Paul Fortress

29 Peter and Paul Fortress seen from
the Trinity Bridge at night

*Each of Petersburg's bridges
has its own distinctive structure
and appearance. They are
humpbacked and elegant, large
and small, subtle and imposing.
Their decorative wrought iron
railings and lamps, coupled with
the granite embankments, give
the face of the city a charming
and inimitable look.
Only two of the bridges over
the Fontanka have retained
their original appearance:
the Chernyshov Bridge (now
known as the Lomonosov
Bridge) and the Staro-Kalinkin
Bridge. Even in these cases, only
the basic architectural form
remains, while the technical
essence has been lost. The towers
of the former house a drawing
mechanism: the middle section
was originally made of wood
and could be raised to let tall
vessels pass.
Equally beautiful and elegant
was the Egyptian Bridge over the
Fontanka. On 20 January 1905,
it collapsed unexpectedly while
a troop of horse-guardsmen was
crossing. It was not reconstructed
until 1956, this time using
a different structural principle.
The bridge lost most of its earlier
majesty, and only the enigmatic
sphinxes have resumed their
positions together with the
obelisks at each of the four
corners.*

30 View of the Neva and the Peter
and Paul Fortress from the spit
of Vasilievsky Island

→
31 Panoramic view of the Neva
and Vasilievsky Island

After it had been decreed, in 1712, that the imperial court was to move from Moscow to the banks of the Neva, the northern city began to be developed in accordance with a plan that had been drawn up previously by local and foreign experts. Pride of place was given to the main waterway, the Neva. The abundance of water and the open skies above the flat, cheerless banks of the river, broken by the mouths of countless smaller channels, set the tone for the architectural development of Petersburg and determined its regular layout.

The Neva became the main "street", and houses were erected in a single row along its banks, following the line of the river as it snaked along its course. The fundamental principle of orderliness and regularity was likewise applied during the development of the city centre. Moreover, in response to a proposal from Peter himself, the architect Domenico Trezzini developed three types of building for the three main social groups within the population of Petersburg, making the buildings of approximately equal height. The skyline created by these almost uniform structures seemed to mirror the long straight lines of the natural landscape.

Vasilievsky Island was originally intended to become the heart of the emerging city. Peter was particularly fond of Amsterdam and hoped that the new capital would somehow remind him of that place. It was planned to create a network of streets and canals, which would drain the marshy land, on Vasilievsky Island. Although this project was not brought to completion, the right-angled arrangement of the streets and the three main avenues which form the architectural basis of the area today almost coincides with the initial plan. The so-called Bolshoy (Large), Sredny (Medium), and Maly (Small) Prospekts run from west to east and are intersected from north to south by 34 "lines". The vista of each of these lines opens out onto the Neva.

The island is shaped like an irregular triangle, the eastern tip of which divides the river into two branches,

VASILIEVSKY ISLAND

32 Spit of Vasilievsky Island seen from the Palace Embankment

→
33 Naval Museum. Inside the former Stock Exchange (1805–1816, architect: Jean-François Thomas de Thomon)

34 Rostral Column. 1805–1810, sculptors: Georges Camberlain, François Thibault. 1810, architect: Jean-François Thomas de Thomon

the Bolshaya and the Malaya Neva. For a hundred years this was the site of the city's port. At the beginning of the 19th century, it was moved further downstream, and now only the wrought iron rings set in the granite walls of the embankment serve as a reminder of the fact that ships once moored here. The spit of Vasilievsky Island was designed to reflect Petersburg's status as an international centre of shipping and commerce. The centrepiece of the resulting architectural composition is the Stock Exchange (1805–1816, architect: Jean-François Thomas de Thomon), which resembles a Doric-style temple, hence its nickname the "Russian Parthenon". The main façade, overlooking the Neva, is adorned with the figures of the sea god Neptune and his retinue, while on the western side an allegorical embodiment of Navigation stands alongside the god of commerce, Mercury. Although Mercury is no longer worshipped here, the building remains faithful to the fierce god of the sea: today, the Stock Exchange is the home of the Naval Museum.

The Stock Exchange is flanked on either side by two warehouses (1826–1832, architect: Giovanni Luchini)

35 Institute of Russian Literature ("Pushkin House")
The former Customs House (1829–1832, architect: Giovanni Luchini)

36 View of the University Embankment from the Admiralty
Academy of Sciences. 1783–1789, architect: Giacomo Quarenghi
Kunstkammer. 1718–1734, architects: Georg Mattarnovi,
Gaetano Chiaveri and Mikhail Zemtsov

in which goods delivered to the city by sea were once stored. Nowadays, the Southern Warehouse is occupied by the Zoological Museum, while the Northern Warehouse houses the Soil Research Institute. Behind them stands the Customs House (1829–1832, architect Giovanni Luchini), which looks out onto the Malaya Neva. In 1927 this building, now familiarly known as "Pushkin House", was given to the Institute of Russian Literature of the Academy of Sciences. A marble statue of Mercury atop the pediment serves as a reminder of the building's original purpose.

On the tip of the island, which was artificially enlarged with deposits of earth, stands a pair of Rostral Columns (1810, architect: Jean-François Thomas de Thomon), symbols of Russia's dominion over the sea. At the foot of these columns sit allegorical statues of Russia's four major trade routes, the Neva, the Volkhov, the Volga and the Dnieper, which for centuries have linked the Baltic with the Caspian and the Black Sea. The torches on the Rostral Columns no longer light the way for sailors hurriedly unloading their ships on dark autumn evenings, but are ignited on public holidays as part of the city's festive illuminations.

37 Menshikov Palace. 1710s–1720s, architects: Giovanni Mario Fontana, Gottfried Johann Schaedel

38 Menshikov Palace. Grand Hall

39 Unknown 18th century artist. *Portrait of Alexander Menshikov*

40 Menshikov Palace. Menshikov's Walnut Study

In the early 18th century, the city's first and largest estate, the property of Peter I's close associate and the first governor of Petersburg, Alexander Menshikov, was built. Today, only the palace remains, overlooking the Neva and equipped with its own pier. The only one of its kind in Petersburg at the time, the palace was used to receive ambassadors and host the Petersburg "assemblies" at which Peter the Great taught European etiquette to the boyars who had moved north from Moscow. Menshikov's life ended in tragedy. In 1727, two years after the death of the first Russian Emperor, he was stripped of his rank and wealth and banished from Petersburg with his family. Menshikov soon died in exile. His palace was confiscated and turned over to the state.

The square is particularly striking when viewed from the air. From above, the brilliance and splendour of the architectural plan are readily apparent. Like the bow of a huge ship, the spit of Vasilievsky Island cleaves the waves of the river as if entering a harbour, marked to the right and left by the golden spires of the Admiralty and the Peter and Paul Fortress.

Contrary to Peter's wishes, Vasilievsky Island did not become the centre of Petersburg. The river, wide and restless, particularly in the autumn, became a serious hindrance, hampering the link between the island and the mainland of the northern capital.

Nonetheless, the architectural idea that was first conceived and partly realised in the development of this area of Petersburg became the guiding aesthetic principle for the entire city. From 1724 to 1734, the building known as the Twelve Collegia was constructed on Vasilievsky Island (architect: Domenico Trezzini). The first major administrative establishment in the city, it was intended to house the twelve different government departments, a fact that was reflected in its unique architectural design. The ground floor gallery, which stretches for almost 400 metres, joins the individual sections of the building, each of which originally had its own door. Today, the building has a single entrance. Since 1819, it has been occupied by the University of Petersburg. The entire embankment, which consisted

41 Academy of Arts. 1764–1788,
architects: Jean-Baptiste Vallin de La Mothe,
Alexander Kokorinov

42 University Embankment. Pier in front of the Academy
of Arts.1832–1834, architect: Konstantin Thon
Sphinx (Egypt, 13th century BC)

The Classical style first emerged in Petersburg architecture in the design of the Academy of Arts (1764–1788, architects: Jean-Baptiste Vallin de La Mothe and Alexander Kokorinov), which stands at the furthest end of the University Embankment and plays an important role in the architectural ensemble on the banks of the Neva. The building was erected after the founding of the Academy (1757) on the site of the houses of Petrine dignitaries, which were bought from their owners. For a number of years, classes were actually held in these homes. The Petersburg Academy of Arts was the first educational establishment of its type in Russia. To this day, Russian artists, sculptors and architects are trained there.

In the early 19th century, a flight of granite steps leading down to the water was created in front of the Academy after designs by the architect Konstantin Thon. Since 1834, the stretch of embankment before the majestic bulk of the Academy of Arts has been guarded by a pair of sphinxes with the face of Amenhotep III, who was in power when the kingdom of Egypt was flourishing. These "enigmatic creatures, the product of a bygone era, a distant country and an alien people, seem completely at home here on the Neva banks, rearing up from the waters of the great river of the northern capital to guard the treasures of its palaces" (Nikolai Antsiferov).

43   Rumiantsev Obelisk in the Rumiantsev Gardens. 1799, architect: Vincenzo Brenna, sculptor: Pierre-Louis Agie

44 Academy of Arts Museum
Vestibule

45 Academy of Arts Museum
Copies of antique sculptures

The old part of Vasilievsky Island is a unique monument to the 18th century. More than any other region of Petersburg, it reflects the architectural plans of the Petrine era. Not only the public buildings, including houses of worship, but the many residential buildings too have more or less retained their original appearance. St Andrew's Cathedral (1764–1780, architect: Alexander Vist), on the corner of Bolshoy Prospect and the sixth line, is particularly remarkable. This wooden cathedral was the first church in Russia to be dedicated to an order. Following the common practice in all European countries, Peter founded a supreme order of state, known as the Order of St Andrew, the apostle who, as legend has it, brought Christianity to pagan Rus. Apart from the Russian Emperors and their heirs, dignitaries of the highest rank were decorated with this order for acts of great merit. St Andrew's Cathedral was rebuilt in stone after the original building was destroyed by fire in 1761. Inside, a carved wooden iconostasis of great artistic value can be seen to this day.

46 St Andrew's Cathedral
1764–1780, architect: Alexander Vist

47 Lieutenant Schmidt Bridge
and the English Embankment
seen from the Lieutenant Schmidt
Embankment

→

48 Lieutenant Schmidt Embankment
Statue of Admiral Krusenstern. 1873,
sculptor: Ivan Schroeder

49 International Cutty Sark Tall Ships'
Races on the Neva

of two parts in the 18th century (the Academy and the Cadet Embankments), became known as the University Embankment. The Twelve Collegia stands perpendicular to the embankment itself. The first building to be constructed facing the Neva during the Petrine era was the *Kunstkammer* (1718–1734, architects: Georg Mattarnovi, Gaetano Chiaveri and Mikhail Zemtsov), which became the city's first public museum. It is now the home of the Peter the Great Museum of Ethnography and Anthropology. The building's central section is crowned with a tower, which naturally brought a sense of variety to the emerging face of this particular bank of Vasilievsky Island.

The compact and regular edifice of the Academy of Sciences with its austere façade, mighty eight-column portico and double staircase so typical of Petersburg clearly illustrates the principles of Classicism, the dominant architectural style of the late 18th – early 19th century. Further down the embankment, the Mining Institute (1806–1811, architect: Andrei Voronikhin) is a monument to Late Classicism, the next stage in the development of this style, characterised by the synthesis of architecture and sculpture. Two sculptural groups embodying the philosophical notions behind the building adorn the steps that lead up to the colonnade. To the right is "Pluto Carrying Off Proserpina" (1809–1811, sculptor: Vasily Demut-Malinovsky), and to the left is "Heracles and Antaeus" (1809–1811, sculptor: Stepan Pimenov). The nature of the plastic art with its exaggerated proportions yet expressive lines is in perfect accord with the heavy Doric forms of the building. The Mining Institute has its own museum, which contains a unique geological collection put together over the course of almost three centuries. It now includes over 15 thousand specimens of rocks and minerals as well as assorted items made from precious and coloured stones. One of its most spectacular exhibits is an enormous chunk of malachite from the Urals, which weighs 1,504 kg and was presented to the museum by Catherine II.

50 Mining Institute. 1806–1811, architect: Andrei Voronikhin

51 Mining Institute Museum. Columned Hall. 1820s, architect: Alexei Postnikov

52 The portico of the Mining Institute Ice breaker *Krasin*

In the second half of the 18th century, a new building appeared alongside the *Kunstkammer* – the Academy of Sciences (1783–1789, architect: Giacomo Quarenghi). The Italian architect, Quarenghi, made a valuable contribution to the architecture of Petersburg. Having fallen in love with Russia, he joined his destiny to the country forever: when the Italian government ordered him to return home, Quarenghi refused to obey and was consequently tried *in absentia* and outlawed.

The panorama of the banks of Vasilievsky Island is completed by the majestic façade of the Mining Institute. This edifice was intended to decorate the city's entrance from the sea, and was thus designed to be seen from afar. Its grandi-ose twelve-column portico against the backdrop of a rusti-cated wall is indeed extremely striking from the water.

Opposite the Mining Institute, the famous icebreaker *Krasin*, which took part in an expedition to rescue Umber-to Nobile in the 1930s, is permanently anchored. Today, it is the home of a museum. The portico of the Mining Institute also looks out onto the shipyards of the Baltic Factory, from which new vessels set out to roam the seas.

On Vasilievsky Island, traditions that have come into being over the course of three centuries are perpetuated to this day. From as early as the Petrine era, Vasilievsky Island has been regarded as a centre of the arts and sciences, the permanent abode of Meditation, Knowledge and Creativity.

Petersburg has more bridges than any other city in the world, including Venice, Amsterdam and Stockholm. Today, over three hundred bridges link the forty-two islands that make up Petersburg. Together with the magnificent architectural ensembles, the bridges play an important part in the general makeup of the city. Petersburg can be called a unique museum of bridges. These indispensable structures are not only fine examples of technical achievement, but also works of art in their own right, which reflect the tastes of the various eras. There is a distinct contrast, for example, between the Trinity Bridge with its steel supports concealed by the graceful, fluid lines of the Art Nouveau style, and the Peter the Great (or Bolsheokhtinsky) Bridge with its "bulky, coarse and obtrusive" design.

←
53 White Nights. View of the Neva from the roof of the Winter Palace

←
54 White Nights
Palace Bridge opening

←
55 White Nights
Lieutenant Schmidt Bridge

56 Rainbow over the Neva

→
57 Panoramic view
of the Bolshaya Neva

ne of the defining characteristics of the design of early Petersburg, besides the regularity of the buildings, was a network of open squares linked by the city's embankments and avenues. Some of these, including Arts Square and Ostrovsky Square, owe their basic appearance to the visions of one man, and they strike something of a "matchless architectural chord". Others, such as Palace Square, Senate Square, St Isaac's Square and Suvorov Square, evolved over the course of a century yet still create the impression of an organic architectural whole.

In 1704, on Admiralty Island, situated on the left bank of the Neva and bordered to the south by the Moika, work began on the building of a shipyard that was designed by Peter the Great himself. Together with the Peter and Paul Fortress, the Admiralty Shipyard became one of the city's main architectural features. In the 1730s, the architect Ivan Korobov abandoned the original plans for the Admiralty and replaced the frame-built warehouses with stone buildings. Moreover, he masterminded the construction of a tower with a tall gilded spire (72m high) topped with a weather vane in the shape of a three-sailed frigate.

At the beginning of the 19th century, the Admiralty underwent fundamental reconstruction under the watchful eye of Andrean Zakharov. The Classical architect, while preserving Korobov's original concept, considerably enlarged the building and enhanced its appearance using sculptural designs. The New Admiralty (1806–1819) was envisaged as a unique monument to the Russian fleet, thus its main entrance was given the form of a triumphal arch. Zakharov repeated the motif of the wide archway in the façades of the two symmetrically placed pavilions that face the Neva.

The grand opening of the Admiralty Embankment took place on 7 March 1880. A monument to Peter I, the toiler and ships' carpenter, was later erected on this embankment, whence ships set sail on their maiden voyages (sculptor: Leopold Bernstam).

58 Admiralty. 1806–1819,
architect: Andrean Zakharov

Even in its early years the Admiralty building represented an important element of the overall design of the city and an influential factor in the formation of what was eventually to become the central part of Petersburg. Frantic building work went on around it, resulting in the creation of 11 settlements inhabited by workmen. In the 1730s, a terrible fire razed this district to the ground, and a committee was established to develop a common plan for its redevelopment. It was at this time that the architect Piotr Eropkin proposed the radial layout that characterises the central region of the city today. Two avenues (Nevsky Prospekt and Voznesensky Prospekt) were laid out from the Admiralty alongside an existing thoroughfare (Gorokhovaya Street).

The sculptural embellishments that indicate the purpose served by the Admiralty play an important part in the composition of the building as a whole. The idea of the synthesis of architecture and sculpture was central to Classical design and was first clearly demonstrated in Andrean Zakharov's work. He presented sculpture in all its manifestations, from freestanding statues to sculpted ornament, united by a single theme – the glorification of Russia's

naval prowess. In front of the main entrance, on either side of the triumphal arch, stand the monumental figures of three sea nymphs holding orbs (1812, sculptor: Feodosy Shchedrin). Mounted on high pedestals, they are supposed to symbolise the free passage of the Russian fleet across the globe. On the attic of the lower portion of the Admiralty tower, *The Establishment of a Fleet in Russia* is depicted in high relief. Covering a length of 22 metres this frieze (1812, sculptor: Ivan Terebenev), plays an important visual and symbolic role in the décor of the building. Allegorical figures *(Glory Holding a Flag over the Ocean)*, mythological characters (Neptune, Minerva, Mercury and Vulcan) and historical personages (Peter I) are brought together in the scene of *Neptune Presenting His Trident to the Russian Emperor* against the background of the Peter and Paul Fortress. Statues of the ancient mythological and historical characters Ajax, Achilles, Pyrrhus and Alexander the Great look down from the four corners of the parapet of the Admiralty tower. High above them, atop the tower's columned pavilion, a further 28 statues are to be seen representing the elements, the winds, the seasons, the goddess Isis and the muse Urania. Allegorical scenes decorate the pediments

of the main and side façades. One of the more fascinating and unexpected of these works is the high relief on the eastern right-hand portico showing *Justice Rewarding the Artists' Labours* (1812, sculptor: Ivan Terebenev), in which the Greek goddess presents each craftsman, from the weaver, the glass-blower and the shepherd to the wine-grower and the tiller, a laurel wreath in honour of his deeds.

Even during Andrean Zakharov's lifetime, this magnificent edifice aroused the rapturous praise of his contemporaries. In the words of one such individual: "This important and useful building now numbers amongst the chief ornaments of the capital and may rightly be declared a mammoth testimony to the latest successes of Russian architecture" (Pavel Svinin).

59 Admiralty Embankment
Eastern pavilion of the Admiralty

60 Caravel at the top
of the Admiralty spire

61 Central tower and spire
of the Admiralty

62 High-reliefs on the Admiralty Triumphal Arch. Detail

63 Panoramic view of the Neva from Palace Bridge

→

64 Senate and Synod. 1829–1836, architect: Carlo Rossi

65 Decembrists Square (formerly Senate Square) in winter

66 Decembrists Square (formerly Senate Square)

67 Monument to Peter the Great
(*The Bronze Horseman*). 1782,
sculptor: Etienne-Maurice Falconet

68 Monument to Peter the Great
Detail

From the very beginning, the Admiralty Shipyard was flanked by two squares, Palace Square on the one side and Decembrists Square (formerly Senate Square) on the other. The emergence of the latter was linked to the construction of the first floating bridge, which joined Vasilievsky Island to the mainland. Because of its location, the square had become one of the most important in the city by the mid-1700s. In the late 18th century, Decembrists Square was known as Peter's Square because of the monument to Peter I (the first equestrian statue in Petersburg) that was erected there in 1782. The Senate, the Synod and the Admiralty serve as the striking wings to a stage upon which the main player is the Emperor – Peter the Great – astride his mount. Behind him towers the august edifice of St Isaac's Cathedral

69

The French sculptor Etienne Falconet's most immaculate work of art was immortalised by the great Russian poet, Alexander Pushkin, in "The Bronze Horseman". Falconet's monument to Peter the Great is the centrepiece of Decembrists Square, and its striking outline is clearly visible even from afar. "If a person happens to be in its vicinity on a foul autumn evening when the sky, turned to chaos, presses down towards the earth and fills it with disarray, the river, constrained by granite walls, groans and rages, sudden gusts of wind rock the lanterns and their wavering light sets the surrounding buildings aquiver, he should fix his gaze upon "the Bronze Horseman", turning, in the firelight, to bronze with starkly pronounced and powerful forms. He will sense such a force, a passionate, impetuous force that beckons into the unknown. And the sweeping gesture, prompting the disquieting question: what next, what lies ahead?" (Nikolai Antsiferov). The monument is a sculptural symbol of an entire epoch of Russian history. It fuses the energy and many aspects of the Emperor – Creator, Reformer and Lawmaker – into one. Falconet wrote, "My tsar does not hold a staff; he extends his beneficent right hand over the land he has conquered. He ascends the rock that serves him as a pedestal, an element of the difficulties he has surmounted".
Peter's Square became known as Senate Square in the early 19th century due to the construction of the majestic edifice of the Senate and the Synod (1829–1836).

69 Admiralty Embankment
Statue of Peter the Carpenter
1880, sculptor: Leopold Bernstam

70 Aerial view of St Petersburg

The architect, Carlo Rossi, joined the two government buildings with a magnificent arch stretching across Galernaya Street, and thereby created an integrated architectural composition. The sculptural group "Justice and Piety" atop the archway completes the building's monumental decor. Senate Square was re-christened in 1923, in honour of a key event in the history of Russia. On 14 December 1825, the ranks of demonstrators in the first organised protest for freedom, the Constitution and human rights lined up at the foot of "the Bronze Horseman". The insurgent regiments were gunned down and the uprising suppressed. The five leaders were subsequently executed and the remaining protesters permanently exiled to Siberia. The forms and symbols of Senate Square have become part of both the history and legend of Petersburg. This area of town is particularly attractive on bright winter days, "when the sun shines softly and tenderly upon the square and the trees."

71   St Isaac's Square
Monument to Nicholas I
1856–1859, sculptor: Piotr Klodt,
architect: Auguste Montferrand
St Isaac's Cathedral. 1818–1858,
architect: Auguste Montferrand

like a fitting backdrop. This cathedral serves as the architectural link between two magnificent squares – Decembrists Square and St Isaac's Square.

The building that is to be seen today – the fourth to bear the name of St Isaac's – was built over the course of 40 years (1818–1858) in accordance with designs by the architect Auguste de Montferrand. The cathedral was intended to be the greatest in the Russian Empire. Vast amounts of money and effort were required to construct this building, which stands at a height of 101.5 metres and covers over a hectare of land. It is the fourth largest domed cathedral of its type in the world after St Peter's in Rome, St Paul's in London and Santa Maria dei Fiori in Florence.

Rectangular in shape, the body of the building has four columned porticoes, which make the vast bulk appear even larger than it already is. Pursuant to the Greek canon, the cathedral is surmounted with a large central dome and four smaller domes at each corner. Both inside and out, the building is adorned with sculptures and reliefs. The interior of the cathedral (4,000 sq.m.) boasts a profusion of gilt,

variegated marble, murals and mosaics. The best painters and sculptors of the time contributed to this unusual work of art.

Central to the interior décor of St Isaac's Cathedral is the combination of coloured marbles, malachite, lapis and gilt, which creates a sumptuous setting for the many magnificent sculptures, paintings and mosaics. Some of the most striking decorations are to be seen in the drum of the main dome and the area below it.

72 St Isaac's Cathedral. Central nave

73 St Isaac's Cathedral. Iconostasis Mosaic: *The Last Supper*
1879–1887, designed by Semion Zhivago
→
74 St Isaac's Cathedral. Iconostasis

75 St Isaac's Cathedral. Stained glass window in the chancel: *The Ascension*
1841–1843, designed by Heinrich-Maria Hess

76 St Isaac's Cathedral. Iconostasis. Detail

77 St Isaac's Cathedral. Iconostasis. Mosaic: *St Nicholas*
1855–1862, designed by Timofei Neff

78 St Isaac's Cathedral. Iconostasis. Mosaic: *St Catherine*
1868–1880, designed by Timofei Neff

A number of eminent artists and sculptors of the Academic school of the 19th century had a hand in decorating the cathedral, including Karl Briullov, Fedor Bruni, Piotr Basin and Ivan Vitali, as well as several lesser-known masters. The mosaics inside the cathedral are particularly worthy of note. Due to the difficulty of maintaining a steady temperature within the building, it was originally planned to replace the initial paintings with mosaics. Most of the mosaics to be seen here are remarkable for their technical excellence, a fact that was celebrated at the London International Exhibition in 1862.

While St Isaac's Cathedral was under construction, the square to its south also underwent certain changes and gradually began to take on the appearance it has today.

79 St Isaac's Cathedral. Central dome

80 Dome of St Isaac's Cathedral

81 St Isaac's Cathedral. Interior. Detail

ХРАМЪ МОИ ХРАМЪ МОЛИТВЫ НАРЕЧЕТСЯ

Between 1856–1859, a monument was erected to Nicholas I in the centre of St Isaac's Square. Once again, the artist responsible was Montferrand. The lamps were designed by the architect Veigelt, and the low fence surrounding the pedestal was the work of Ludwig Bonshmedt. The artists Nikolai Ramazanov and Robert Zaleman took part in the creation of the sculpture, producing the somewhat naturalistic reliefs and the female figures on the pedestal. These allegorical characters, which resemble Nicholas I's wife and daughters, symbolise the Christian virtues: Faith (with the cross and the Gospels), Wisdom (holding a mirror), Justice (bearing the scales), and Might (with a lance and shield). The model of the equine statue itself was made by Piotr Klodt, who personally participated in the casting of it. The sculptor's precise mathematical calculations made it possible to use just two points of support in the mounting of the horse. The resulting sculptural group creates a striking effect when viewed from any point on the square or the neighbouring streets. The masterful execution of the central statue together with the monument's fortuitous location make it a work of genuine artistic value.

82 St Isaac's Cathedral. Autumn

83 View of the monument to Nicholas I and the Mariinsky Palace from St Isaac's Cathedral

In 1817–1820, the magnificent Lobanov-Rostovsky residence, designed by Auguste Montferrand, was built to the east of what was then the third building of St Isaac's Cathedral. This enormous edifice in the shape of a regular triangle occupies an entire block between St Isaac's Square, Admiralty Boulevard and Voznesensky Prospekt. Its façade, overlooking the Admiralty, is decorated with a grand portico mounted on the ground floor arcade.

On the eastern side of the square, stand two buildings, the hotels *Astoria* and *Angleterre* (where the Russian poet Sergei Yesenin took his own life). The *Astoria*, on the corner of Bolshaya Morskaya Street, was erected on the site of some early residential buildings. When the architect Fedor Lidval submitted his plans for the future hotel in 1911, he was ordered to cut off a corner of the building and make it no higher than one floor, otherwise it would obstruct the wonderful view of the square that was to be had from the street.

84 Mariinsky Palace. 1839–1844,
architect: Andrei Stackenschneider

85 Timofei Neff. 1805–1876
Portrait of Grand Princess Maria Nikolaevna. 1850–1860

86 Mariinsky Palace. Church of St Nicholas

87 Mariinsky Palace. Main Staircase

88 Mariinsky Palace. Red Room

In the 1840s the square was enlarged when the state purchased five houses on Bolshaya Morskaya Street and had them replaced with two symmetrical buildings designed by the architect Nikolai Efimov for the Ministry of State Property. St Isaac's Square also embraced the Blue Bridge, the widest in Petersburg (97.3 metres) and the former Mariinskaya Square. The appearance of the latter was dictated by the Mariinsky Palace (1839–1844), which was constructed on the site of a building dating from the 18th century. The architect, Andrei Stackenschneider, incorporated the entire central block of the previous building by Vallin de La Mothe into the body of the new palace, but changed the entrance on the main façade to give it the appearance of an open arcade. This palace was intended as a wedding present for Nicholas I's eldest daughter, Maria. Today, the palace is occupied by the City Council. St Isaac's Square is intersected by Bolshaya Morskaya Street. Unlike the majority of the city's main avenues, the street is not straight because it follows the bends of the Moika. By the mid-19th century, many of the existing residential buildings on Bolshaya Morskaya had been significantly renovated, and by the end of the century the district was unofficially known as "the City" due to the many banks and offices located there. The late 18th century residences were preserved and some of them welcomed cultural and social organisations under their roofs, such as the current house of the Composers' Union. In the 1790s, a three-storey wing was added to the building. In 1834, it was bought by the architect Auguste de Montferrand, who enlivened the right-hand section of the façade with motifs from Renaissance architecture, embellishing it with three friezes, while on the left-hand side he built a high terrace. A splendid staircase of white marble, decorated with candelabras of gilded bronze, was installed in 1873 (architect: Ivan Strom). The surviving interior décor dates back to the 19th century.

89 Former Demidov Mansion
1836–1840, architect: Auguste Montferrand

90 Former Demidov Mansion
Winged figures of Glory bearing a shield with a coat of arms. 1840–1850

Palace Square did not gain its title until the middle of the 18th century, when the Winter Palace (1754–1762, architect: Bartolomeo Francesco Rastrelli), the home of the Russian Emperors from 1763 to 1917, was built along the northern edge overlooking the Neva. Today, the Winter Palace is one of the five buildings that make up the architectural ensemble of the State Hermitage Museum.

In 1764, Catherine II ordered the construction of a new building to house her rapidly expanding collection of artworks. Thus, the Small Hermitage (1764–1775) was built onto the Winter Palace. This building, dating from the time of early Classicism, has two façades. The main façade, which looks out over the Neva, was the work of Jean-Baptiste Vallin de La Mothe. The three-storey wing facing Millionnaya Street was designed by Yury Velten, who linked the two parts of the building with a hanging winter garden on the first floor. Further along the embankment, beyond the Small Hermitage, stands the Old Hermitage (1771–1787), also built by Velten. The name "Old Hermitage" came about in the mid-19th century after the construction of the monumental New Hermitage (1839–1852, architect: Leo von Klenze) on the Millionnaya Street side for the growing gallery, which was finally declared a "public museum" in 1852. The front of the building is decorated with the figures of ten Atlantes, each of which was hewn from a single block of grey granite after a model by the sculptor Alexander Terebenev.

The New Hermitage is one of the very few buildings in the history of architecture that have been built specially for the purposes of a museum. It is because of this that the premises, in which the architect achieved a surprising harmony between the interior design and the works of art preserved there, are particularly interesting. The Hall of Twenty Columns, otherwise known as the Greco-Etruscan Vase Hall, the three magnificent rooms of the Large and Small Skylight Halls for exhibiting paintings, the Aura Room in which antique sculpture is displayed, and the Modern Sculpture Rooms are all

91 Palace Embankment
Winter Palace. 1754–1762, architect:
Bartolomeo Francesco Rastrelli

In 1818–1819, the grandiose, semicircular, Empire style façade of the General Staff building (architect: Carlo Rossi) took shape on the southern side of Palace Square. Opposite the central point of the long straight façade of the Winter Palace, the architect erected a Triumphal Arch, crowned with the chariot of Victory and decorated with statues of warriors (sculptors: Stepan Pimenov and Vasily Demut-Malinovsky). This arch links two buildings, the General Staff building and the Ministry of Foreign Affairs and Finance. It spans the width of Bolshaya Morskaya Street, which approaches the square at an angle and thus prompted Rossi to install two extra arches on the street side. In 1843, the Headquarters of the Guards were completed on the eastern side of the square (architect: Alexander Briullov). This building provided a harmonious complement to the Palace Square ensemble, which is unsurpassed in all Petersburg.

In 1834, in honour of the twenty-year victory over Napoleon, the Alexander Column, a 40 metre high pillar of granite topped by the figure of an angel with the face of Alexander I, was erected in the centre of the square (architect: Auguste de Montferrand, sculptor: Boris Orlovsky).

92   Palace Square
Alexander Column
1834, architect: Auguste Montferrand, sculptor: Boris Orlovsky

General Staff building
1818–1819, architect: Carlo Rossi

especially worthy of note. Many of them are decorated with columns, reliefs and murals, and have mosaic floors.

Besides the buildings in which artworks are exhibited, the Hermitage complex includes the Hermitage Theatre (1783–1786, architect: Giacomo Quarenghi), which is linked to the Old Hermitage by a gallery spanning the Winter Canal.

The interiors of the Winter Palace, with rare exceptions, have not retained their original appearance: in 1837 they fell victim to a terrible fire. Nonetheless, the Winter Palace's main staircase (known as the Ambassadorial or Jordan Staircase), a sweeping, white marble affair with twin flights, still looks the way it did when it was installed in the 18th century.

The monolithic granite columns, painted ceiling, sculptures, intricate stuccowork and abundance of gilt and mirrors make it at once vibrant, elegant and majestic.

The St George Hall or Large Throne Room (1795, architect: Giacomo Quarenghi) was restored by Vasily Stasov in 1842. This two-tone room with an area of 800 square metres

has a distinctly august and ceremonial appearance due to the white marble columns around its perimeter and its two rows of splendid bronze chandeliers. On the wall above the throne is a marble bas-relief depicting *St George Slaying the Dragon*. The parquet floor is made of 16 types of wood.

The Hermitage possesses original works and has very few copies. Occasionally, however, copies may be of considerable interest. The gallery built by Giacomo Quarenghi in 1783–1792 is a copy of the Raphael Loggias. A *loggia* is an Italian word meaning an open gallery. The loggias of the Vatican Palace were built by Donato d'Agnolo Bramante and decorated under the guidance of Raphael by his pupils in the fresco technique. The paintings were copied by order of Catherine

93 Alexander Column. Bas-relief
1834, sculptors: Ivan Leppe, Piotr Svintsov

94 Palace Square. View from
the arch of the General Staff building

92

The Winter Palace was built in
the sumptuous and ornate style
of the Baroque, characteristic
for its diversity, dynamism
and expressiveness.
By design, the palace constitutes
a quadrangle with a large
central courtyard. The latter
was entered from the square
through a pair of enormous
wrought iron gates. The profusion of columns and pilasters
along the façades, the riot of
sculptures on the roof in the
form of urns and female figures,
and the many and variform
windows embellished with small
pediments, combined with a
generous helping of gilt, lend the
building an opulent and exu-
berant appearance. The Winter
Palace is undoubtedly the jewel
in the crown of the square, and
it introduces a rather "playful
tone" into the otherwise stern
and conservative atmosphere
created by the buildings
of Carlo Rossi.

95 Panorama of Palace Square

→
96 Winter Palace. Main Staircase
(Jordan Staircase). 1754–1762,
architect: Bartolomeo Rastrelli;
1838–1839, architect: Vasily Stasov

97 Winter Palace. St George Hall
(Large Throne Hall). 1795,
architect: Giacomo Quarenghi;
1842, architect: Vasily Stasov

98 Winter Palace
Peter the Great Hall
1833, architect: Auguste Montferrand;
1842, architect: Vasily Stasov

the Great on pieces of cloth in tempera by a group of artists led by Carlos Unterberger and sent to St Petersburg where they took their place on the walls of a specially built gallery.

In 1783, Catherine II ordered Giacomo Quarenghi to erect a new court theatre on the Palace Embankment. The court architect succeeded in creating a veritable masterpiece – one of the most perfect palatial theatres in Europe. Quarenghi used the ground floor of the former Winter Palace of Peter I as a basement, on which he put up a majestic auditorium and a stage. The auditorium is remarkable for its balanced proportions. Taking the form of the ancient Roman theatre as his model, Quarenghi resolved the rows in the shape of an amphitheatre. The theatre became the favourite resting place of Catherine the Great. Usually the entire royal court, the heir's family and diplomats were present at the performances – up to 200 guests.

99 Fedor Rokotov. 1730s–1808
Portrait of Catherine II
Late 1770s

100 Carl Fabergé. *Imperial regalia*

Although the Hermitage's collection of Italian paintings does not span every period of the country's artistic history, the quality of the works exhibited here and the renown of the men who created them enable it to compete with the world's most famous collections of works by this particular school. Giorgione's "Judith", Raphael's "Madonna Conestabile" and "The Holy Family", Titian's "St Sebastian", Caravaggio's "The Lute Player", Veronese's "Adoration of the Magi" and Tintoretto's "Birth of St John the Baptist" are just a few of the many treasures of the Hermitage. Undoubtedly, two of the best and most famous works are the canvases painted by the great Renaissance artist, Leonardo da Vinci (1452–1519), "The Madonna Benois" and "The Madonna Litta". "The Madonna Benois" was painted in 1478. The date is corroborated by notes that da Vinci himself made amongst the pages of his sketches and writings, which are preserved in the Uffizi in Florence. The young mother is portrayed in an almost secular light as a carefree Florentine woman, the embodiment of earthly beauty and maternal love, playing with her child. This canvas was purchased for the Hermitage in 1914 by Emperor Nicholas II from the family of the architect Leonty Benois. The second canvas, also bearing the name of its owner, Count Litta, from whom it was acquired in Italy in 1865, dates from a later period of the artist's career.

101 Leonardo da Vinci. 1452–1519
*Madonna with a Flower
(Madonna Benois)*. 1478

102 Leonardo da Vinci. 1452–1519
*Madonna and Child
(Madonna Litta)*. c. 1490

The Small, or Peter the Great Throne Room (1833, architect: Auguste Montferrand), also restored by Stasov in 1842, was dedicated to the memory of Peter I. It was intended for small receptions. The walls of the room are covered with velvet embroidered with silver. In a large niche with a rounded vault, a gilded silver throne, made in England, stands on a raised platform. A painting depicting Peter I with the goddess Minerva hangs on the wall (1730s, Jacopo Amiconi). This interior is notable for its unique and lavish design. The décor of the Malachite Room (architect: Alexander Briullov) has been preserved in its entirety. The bronze bases and capitals of the malachite columns, traced with gold, create a striking complement to the gilded doors and ceiling ornaments. The south wall is decorated with murals by the artist Antonio Vighi on the themes of "Day", "Night" and "Poetry". The technique used in the execution of these works was quite extraordinary: they were first painted on calico and then glued to the artificial marble of the walls. The interior of the Boudoir (1850–1860s, architect: Harald Bosse), designed in the style of the Late Rococo, is characterised by elegance, intricate forms and an interesting use of colour. The room is composed of two spaces– a central body and an alcove. By using such a technique, the architect was able to visually alter the proportions of this extremely long room.

103 Winter Palace
Malachite Drawing Room
Late 1830s– early 1840s,
architect: Alexander Briullov

104 Winter Palace. Boudoir
1850s–1860s,
architect: Harald Bosse

105 Small Hermitage
Pavilion Hall. 1850–1858,
architect: Andrei Stackenschneider

The décor of the Pavilion Hall (1850–1858, architect: Andrei Stackenschneider) in the Small Hermitage combines elements of the Renaissance, Classical and Moorish styles. The predominance of white, the splendour of the gilded bronze chandeliers with their crystal pendants, the murmur of the fountains, and the light streaming through the windows make it one of the palace's most memorable interiors.

One of the highlights of the museum, an 18th century clock ("Peacock") made by the English mechanic James Cox, is to be found in the Pavilion Hall. The clock first appeared in Russia in 1780 and was purchased by Prince Grigory Potemkin as a gift for Catherine II. The clock itself had been dismantled, and only one Ivan Kulibin succeeded in putting it back together again. This curious plaything, intended for decoration and amusement, is an intricate mechanism comprising the clockwork figures of a peacock, a cockerel, an owl and a squirrel. The dial itself is hidden in an aperture in the cap of a mushroom. When the clock is wound up, the melodious tinkling of little bells can be heard, after which the peacock spreads its tail feathers and the cockerel crows.

The Gold Drawing Room (1839, architect: Alexander Briullov) gained its name in the 1850s because of its golden walls and sumptuous gilded furniture. The room's bright walls were originally covered with gilded stuccowork in the form of tendrils and palmettes.

106 Small Hermitage. Pavilion Hall
The *Peacock* Clock
Late 18th century,
craftsman: James Cox

107 Winter Palace
Golden Drawing Room. 1839,
architect: Alexander Briullov

It is generally believed that the Hermitage was established as a museum in 1764, when Catherine II purchased a collection belonging to the merchant Johann Gotzkowsky, which included 225 canvases by renowned Western European masters. Today, the Hermitage collection, which has been put together over the course of more than two centuries, numbers over two million exhibits. The Hermitage's Special Collection contains items made from precious metals by craftsmen who lived over two or three thousand years ago. Amongst such unique exhibits are items from the Siberian Collection of Peter the Great. These include many pairs of belt ornaments, elegantly decorated with coloured paste and turquoise and depicting stylised animals mauling their victims. Of particular interest are the articles of Scythian culture dating from the 7th to the 3rd century BC, found during the excavation of burial mounds in the valley of the River Kuban in the Northern Caucasus. The collection includes numerous examples of weaponry, household objects, horse harnesses, devotional articles and various items of golden finery. More specifically, these are the huge gold "Panther" and the famous golden "Deer", which has become one of the symbols of the Hermitage.

108 Raphael's Loggia. 1783—1792, architect: Giacomo Quarenghi

109 Hermitage Theatre. Auditorium. 1783—1786, architect: Giacomo Quarenghi

→

110 Rembrandt Harmensz. van Rijn. 1606—1669
The Return of the Prodigal Son. 1668—1669

111 Old Hermitage. Rembrandt room viewed from the upper landing of the Council Staircase

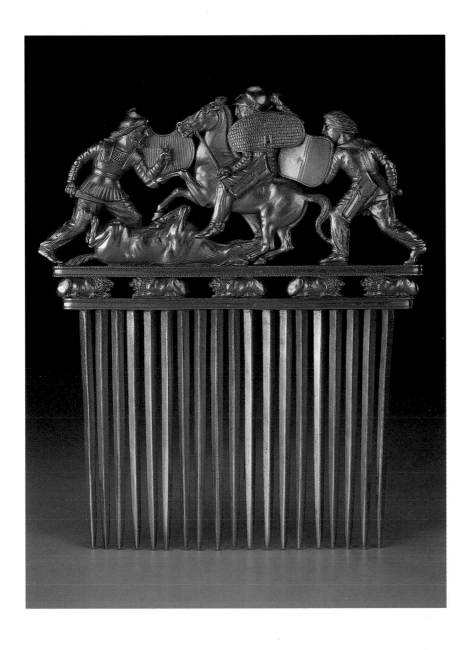

The museum's collection of Western European art is one of the most famous in the world. It encompasses a vast selection of sculptures, drawings, engravings, and items of applied art, but the picture gallery is undoubtedly its most important component.

The collection of Spanish painting contains works by all of the most famous masters of the Golden Age of Spanish art (1580–1680), namely El Greco, José de Ribera, Francisco de Zurbarán, Diego Velázquez and Bartolomé Esteban Murillo. The art of Murillo was especially popular in Russia in the 18th century. The artist's fame inspired Catherine the Great to purchase a number of his superb canvases for her Hermitage collection. The collection of German paintings is small. Amongst the most interesting exhibits are the works of the Renaissance masters, Lucas Cranach the Elder and Ambrosius Holbein. Painting of the 17th–19th century is represented by canvases by Anton Raffael Mengs and Caspar David Friedrich, artists of the Classical and Romantic schools respectively. The Hermitage collection of Flemish and Dutch art is one of the greatest in the world. Worthy of special note among several works by the Old

116

Netherlandish Masters acquired by the Hermitage during the reign of Catherine the Great was the tryptich *The Healing of the Blind Man of Jericho* by Lucas van Leyden, but the major part of Netherlandish "primitives" appeared in Russia thanks to 19th-century art collectors. The art of Flanders is exhaustively represented in the Hermitage. Its collection includes over 500 works in a variety of genres demonstrating the versatile mastery of Flemish artists – multifigure compositions of mythological, allegorical and religious content, portraits, still lifes, landscapes and everyday scenes. The collection makes it possible to illustrate all the specific features of one of the leading 17th-century schools of art that contains more than 140 names. The museum owns forty-two works by the leader of the Flemish school, Peter Paul Rubens. The best of these are *The Union of Earth and Water*, *Perseus and Andromeda*, and *Bacchus*, depicting Rubens' favourite theme from ancient mythology. Elements of Rubens' style can also be seen in the paintings of other leading Flemish artists such as Frans Snyders, Anthony van Dyck and Jacob Jordaens. The first paintings by Dutch artists appeared in St Petersburg long before the foundation of the Hermitage. Nowhere else beyond

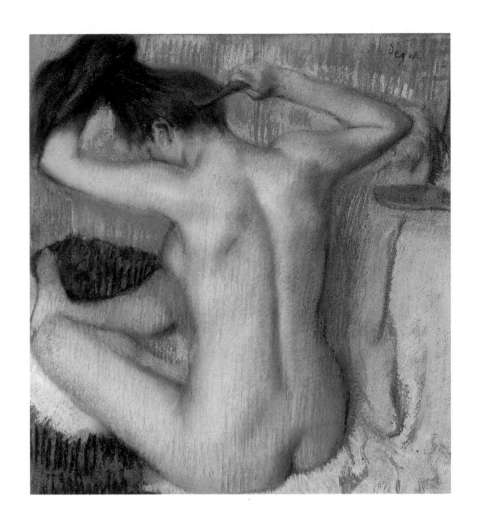

The second floor of the Winter Palace houses an exhibition of late 19th – early 20th century French painting. The Hermitage's collection of Impressionist and Post-Impressionist works is famed throughout the world. It is comprised largely of canvases once owned by the early 20th century private collectors, Sergei Shukin and Ivan Morozov, both of whom lived in Moscow. The works by Claude Monet, Camille Pissarro, Alfred Sisley and Pierre-Auguste Renoir that are to be found in the Hermitage date from the heyday of Impressionist painting. The Impressionist artists discovered new ways of conveying the direct impressions created by nature. They were fascinated by the ability of light to miraculously alter the shape and colour of an object. Paul Cezanne, Vincent van Gogh and Paul Gauguin were also active around the time of Monet, Pissarro and Renoir. Having explored the techniques of Impressionist art, they went on to develop a new style that is commonly known as Post-Impressionism. The search for new means of expression led them to an interpretation of artistic forms that subsequently gave rise to the avant-garde art of the 20th century.

125   Paul Cézanne. 1839–1906
Still Life with Curtain. c. 1899

126   Vincent van Gogh. 1853–1890
Ladies of Arles. 1888

127   Pierre-Auguste Renoir. 1841–1919
Girl with a Fan. 1881

128   Paul Gauguin. 1848–1903
Woman Holding a Fruit. 1893

129   Pierre Bonnard. 1867–1947
Evening in Paris. 1911

the borders of Holland is the Dutch school represented with such completeness as in the Hermitage. A special feature of the collection, besides its huge size (over 1000 paintings) and a number of recognized masterpieces, is that the great masters – Frans Hals, Adriaen van Ostade, Gerard Terborch, Willem Claesz Heda, Willem Kalf, Jacob van Ruisdael– are displayed here amidst less prominent artists whose works are sometimes rare even in Dutch collections. Most of the artists painted village brawls and the everyday life of wealthy citizens, as well as landscapes and still lifes, astonishing for their delicacy and rich texture. The Hermitage collection of works by Rembrandt, Holland's great artistic genius, can be called unique without any reservation. More than twenty paintings represent various phases in the master's complicated career which lasted forty years. Created in different years, Rembrandt's paintings *The Sacrifice of Abraham, Flora, David and Jonathan, Danae, The Holy Family* and *The Portrait of an Old*

Man in Red are his most important works, eloquently expressing his creative credo. The painting *The Return of the Prodigal Son* occupies a place of its own in Rembrandt's legacy. It is a great summation of his thoughts on the sense of life and the utmost evocation of his pictorial mastery. The Hermitage's world-famous French collection, which is deservedly considered the pride of the museum, contains many masterpieces of painting, sculpture and applied art of the fifteenth to the twentieth century. It fills more than fifty rooms of the Winter Palace and represents practically all the styles and trends of French art. Works by nearly every major French artist can be found there. There is no collection outside France capable of rivaling the Hermitage in the quantity and quality of superb

130 Henri Matisse. 1869–1954. *Dance.* 1910

131 New Hermitage. Portico with Atlantes. 1848, architect: Leo von Klenze, sculptor: Alexander Terebenev

examples of painting, sculpture and decorative art. It is difficult even to enumerate all the French painters whose works are on display in the Hermitage, but it is sufficient to mention pictures by such celebrated artists as Poussin, Watteau, Fragonard, Delacroix, Monet, Renoir, Cézanne and Matisse.

Visitors to Petersburg will not forget the elegant bridge that spans the quiet waters of the Winter Canal, linking the Old Hermitage with the Hermitage Theatre. Originally, this bridge arched so steeply that tall carriages leaned violently as they passed and almost toppled over, while in later days a car travelling at high speed would have taken off from the ground as it went over the bridge. Thus, in the 20th century, the height of the arc was altered. The bow of the bridge reflects the curved wall of the "squat yellow tower that supports the arch of the palace, from beneath which the wide river can be seen, covered with faintly whispering ice-floes like a flock of swans slowly completing their journey, and, on the far side of the river, the walls of the sombre fortress, above which a shining spire has been raised, crowned with an archangel" (Nikolai Antsiferov).

132 View of the Hermitage complex from the Palace Bridge

133 Winter Canal

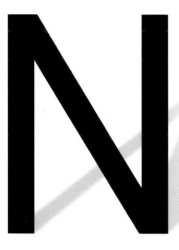

Nevsky Prospekt, as straight as an arrow, is Petersburg's main street. Although it began to take shape within the first ten years of the city's existence, it developed very slowly because the attention of town planners and architects alike was centred first and foremost on the banks of the Neva and Vasilievsky Island as the intended heart of the emerging city.

The new capital became deserted after Peter I died, but gained a new lease of political life when Anna Ioannovna came to the throne. Building work was also revived. As a consequence of Piotr Yeropkin's famous plan to make the "trident" the basis for the layout of the city, the area between the Admiralty and the Moika became the new centre of the capital. In 1738, one of the "radial avenues" starting from the tower of the Admiralty was officially christened "Nevsky Prospekt" and declared Petersburg's main street.

Thenceforth, Nevsky Prospekt was the centre of much architectural activity, and over the course of the next one and a half centuries it took on the appearance it has today. The street is characterised by a sense of proportionality and integrity. Although it comprises buildings from different eras, they are all of more or less the same height. This is because of a decree issued in 1762 upon the completion of the Winter Palace, which stated that no stone buildings were to be made taller than the palace itself. On the roof of the latter stood a small tower from which signals were given to indicate that the ruling elite was departing for its country residences, and nothing was to conceal this mechanism.

Nevsky Prospekt intersects a number of rivers and canals. The bridges spanning these are a characteristic feature of Petersburg. The city boasts a number of "antique" bridges, which have maintained their original appearance. These are to be found in the centre of the northern capital, joining the banks of the former Krivusha River. At the time of Catherine II, the river was lined with granite and named the Catherine Canal, although locals referred it to simply as the *kanava* (ditch). The latter runs resolutely between plain streets and gloomy

134 Anichkov Bridge. Sculptural group: *The Taming of the Horse* 1841–1850, sculptor: Piotr Klodt

By the end of the 19th century, Nevsky Prospekt had become the commercial and financial centre of bourgeois Petersburg. The appearance of the street began to change as increasing numbers of banks, offices, insurance firms and stock companies moved in. Heads of businesses sought to purchase or rent premises on the city's main thoroughfare. The more affluent amongst them, however, bought plots of land, tore down the existing buildings and commissioned architects to design new premises in the style of the times. These properties, built using the latest technology, were supposed not only to promote the image of the company as a respectable and prosperous venture, but also to meet changing aesthetic demands. A splendid illustration of this is the building on the corner of Nevsky Prospekt and Griboedov Canal (1902–1904, architect: Pavel Suzor), the one-time home of the famous sewing machine manufacturers, Singer. This multi-storey construction of glass and metal, crowned with a globe that symbolises the spread of the company's product throughout the world, is a unique example of the architecture of the day.

Suzor's tower became a popular symbol of 20th century St Petersburg, which by then was not only the capital of the empire, but also the principal city of one of the strongest and most advanced world powers. Today, the building is known as "Dom Knigi" ("The House of Books") because of its current tenants – St Petersburg's largest bookshop, which sells all kinds of printed matter.

135 View of Nevsky Prospekt and Griboedov Canal from Kazan Cathedral. Singer building (House of Books). 1902–1904, architect: Pavel Suzor

136 Singer building. Sculptural group on top of the tower. 1902–1904, sculptors: Ober, Adamson

buildings, while the ghosts of Nikolai Gogol and Fedor Dostoevsky's heroes seem to haunt the narrow, dark, stone passageways and roam the countless courtyards on either side.

Now known as Griboedov Canal, the river makes its way beneath an incredible number of bridges. Of all twenty of these, the most striking are the Lion Bridge and the Bank Bridge (both built in 1825–26), which owe their unique appearance and fantastic ornaments to the architect Walter Traitteur and the sculptor Pavel Sokolov.

Bank Bridge, a pedestrian suspension bridge that is the narrowest in the city (1.85 metres), is situated in front of the former Assignment Bank (now occupied by the University of Economics and Finance). At either end sit pairs of griffins –

mythical creatures in the form of winged lions. Stories and legends describe these beasts as reliable guardians of treasure, making them an apt choice for this particular location.

On Nevsky Prospekt only a very few 18th-century buildings are to be seen in their original guise, one of which stands on the corner of the Moika beside the Green Bridge. The Stroganov Palace (1752–1754) is one of the few examples of the private residences designed by Rastrelli. The building blends

137 Griboedov Canal. Bank Bridge
1825–1826, engineer: Walter Traitteur,
sculptor: Pavel Sokolov

138 Bank Bridge. Griffins

in organically with the remainder of the block. In the centre of its façade, facing the main street, is a pair of gates that lead into the inner courtyard. Originally, all of the entrances to the building were located in here. Inside, a grand staircase led to the first floor where the staterooms were located. Today, the Stroganov Palace is inhabited by a branch of the Russian Museum, and major restoration projects are underway to restore the once magnificent interiors.

The then huge three-storey palace is a reminder of the splendour of Elizabeth Petrovna's reign and the inordinate wealth of the Stroganovs, who owned "half of the Urals" and 25,000 serfs. The owner of the palace, Alexander Sergeevich, received an excellent technical education abroad and, while travelling around Italy, became fascinated by the arts and began to purchase a variety of works. He built up an extensive collection of paintings, engravings, coins and items of applied

art. Having significant resources at his disposal, Stroganov also sponsored writers, musicians and poets. Because of his knowledge of art, the count was made an honorary member of the Academy of Arts in 1768 and elected president of the Academy in 1800. When Stroganov's wife fell in love and left her family, the count entrusted the upbringing of his only son, Paul, entirely to the latter's French tutor. Paul Alexandrovich was in France at the time of the Revolution and, under the influence of his governor, began to sympathise with the insurgents. At Catherine II's insistence, Paul's father urged the boy to leave mutinous France and return home at once. Stroganov the Younger was accompanied on his journey by a young man by the name of Andrei Voronikhin from one of the families in bondage to his father.

139 Kazan Cathedral. 1801–1811, architect: Andrei Voronikhin

The colonnade that conceals the main bulk of the Cathedral of the Kazan Icon of the Mother of God lends the entire building an unusual combination of gracefulness and majesty. The monumental portals at either end resemble vast gateways.

The elegance and august simplicity of the interior of the cathedral is also quite stunning. A pair of colonnades divides the interior into three naves, giving it the secular appearance of a room in a palace. The longest and widest of these is the central nave. Above the point at which the central nave meets the transept towers the dome, the first in Russia to be built using metal supports. The light, flooding in through the windows of the dome, makes the cathedral seem very spacious. The monolithic columns of porphyry, with their exquisite bases and capitals traced in bronze, give the interior an air of formal grandeur just as the architect had intended.

Russia's best sculptors and painters were enlisted to decorate the Kazan Cathedral and transformed it into a "temple of Russian art".

For several decades, the building was occupied by the Museum of Religion and Atheism. Consequently, only a few icons and precious religious artefacts remained within its walls. Now that the cathedral has been returned to the bosom of the Church, it has once again acquired a wealth of items for use in religious ceremony.

140   Kazan Cathedral. Interior

141   Kazan Cathedral. North chapel
Tomb of Field Marshal
Mikhail Kutuzov

→

142   View of the portico and dome
of Kazan Cathedral

143   Kazan Cathedral. Colonnade

As the city's main thoroughfare, Nevsky Prospekt was a hive of commercial activity. Its most serious and respectable shopping arcade was the so-called Gostiny Dvor, which first emerged in its current position in the 1730s. The impressive establishment to be seen there today took 28 years to build, from 1757 to 1785. The original designs by Rastrelli proved extremely costly to realise and were consequently adapted by Vallin de La Mothe. The result was a building of simple splendour and vast proportions: the façade overlooking Nevsky Prospekt is 230 metres in length. The four sides of Gostiny Dvor were named according to the types of goods sold there. Thus two of the wings were referred to as Sukonnaya (Cloth) and Zerkalnaya (Mirrors) respectively, while the other two were known as Bolshaya and Malaya Surovskaya after the expensive fabrics and goods imported from the town of Surozh (now Sudak) on the Black Sea.

The arcade also embodied the essence of the new Nevsky Prospekt, of which it was written: "All that is dazzling, valuable and lavish, all that Petersburg trade and industry can possibly flaunt, is rolled into one here."

Voronikhin later designed the Cathedral of the Kazan Icon of the Mother of God, which stands a short distance away from the Stroganov Palace.

Nevsky Prospekt opens out onto a number of squares, which break the monotony of this otherwise long straight row of buildings. The first and smallest of these squares lies in front of the Kazan Cathedral and is framed by the magnificent semi-circular colonnade of the cathedral itself. The interior of the cathedral is striking for its size and architectural proportions.

Monumental sculpture plays an important part in the building's décor, including the large statues in the porticoes and countless reliefs. The cathedral was named in honour of the holy Kazan Icon of the Mother of God, one of the precious relics of the Russian Orthodox Church that was kept there. Since the cathedral was constructed between 1801–1811, during the time of the Napoleonic campaigns, it became a unique monument to the valour of the Russian army. Field Marshal Mikhail Kutuzov, the man who led the army that

defeated Napoleon in 1812, is buried inside the cathedral. Standards seized from enemy armies decorate the walls. The ensemble of the square is completed by two statues by Boris Orlovsky, erected in front of the cathedral in 1832. These are monuments to Field Marshals Kutuzov and Mikhail Barclay de Tolly, heroes of 1812.

Mikhailovskaya Street joins Nevsky Prospekt with Arts Square (formerly Mikhailovskaya Square), the product of an ingenious piece of urban design by Carlo Rossi. The great ar-chitect transformed the once neglected and empty expanse of the former Summer Gardens into one of the most beautiful places in the city. In accordance with Rossi's plans, Sadovaya Street, which leads towards Mikhailovsky Castle, was extended and became the square's southeast boundary. The two remaining sides of the square were bordered by water: to the northeast ran the Moika, while the Catherine Canal lay to the northwest.

151   Panoramic view of Arts Square

In 1895, the Mikhailovsky Palace was purchased by the state to house the first state museum of national art. In conjunction with this, fundamental alterations were made to the palace interiors. Thus, only a small number of these have retained their original appearance. The vestibule and the main staircase, for example, have barely changed. The most interesting room, however, is the White Hall, where not only the colourful murals, but also the furniture designed by Rossi have been preserved.

The museum officially opened in 1895. At the time, it contained 445 paintings, which were taken from the Academy of Arts Museum, the Hermitage and other palace collections. Thus, the Hermitage contributed the world-famous illustration of "The Last Day of Pompeii" by Karl Briullov, the huge canvas depicting "The Brazen Serpent" by Fedor Bruni, and Ivan Aivazovsky's most celebrated seascape, "The Tenth Wave". These works were to be seen in the large rooms devoted to Academic painting. Here too, exhibits from the Academy of Arts Museum were displayed, including student "programmes" and Diploma Works, such as those of Alexander Ivanov. The museum's collection grew considerably immediately after the revolution and in the 1920s, when private collections were nationalised.

152 Unknown artist
Portrait of Alexander III. 1880–1890

153 Russian Museum
Large Academic Hall. 1999

154 Russian Museum. Upper landing of the Main Staircase. 1819–1825, architect: Carlo Rossi

It was at this time that the splendid collection of late 19th – early 20th century paintings began to take shape. The gems of the exhibit included canvases by Ilya Repin, Vasily Surikov and Mikhail Vrubel. Over the coming years, the museum was to become the owner of the best collection of Russian avant-garde works in the world, acquiring paintings by such widely acclaimed artists as Wassily Kandinsky and Kasimir Malevich. In more recent years, the State Russian Museum has amassed a priceless collection of early Russian art and now has a total of 5,800 icons both on view and in storage. It also boasts an extensive and exquisite collection of drawings and objects of applied art as well as the largest collection of 18th–20th century Russian sculpture in the country, consisting of 4,409 exhibits. The Russian Museum has lately accumulated a significant collection of early Russian artworks. These include such priceless icons as "The Angel with the Golden Hair" and "St George and the Dragon". The first of these is one of the most famous depictions of the Archangel Gabriel, showing the obedient servant of God delivering his message to the Virgin at the Annunciation. The icon of the archangel would once have been found on the central row of an iconostasis, on which Biblical figures were depicted by rank. The Archangels and Angels were considered the highest ranking of the nine "choirs" of supernatural beings that performed the will of God and played a part in the lives of men.

155 Russian Museum. White Hall 1819–1825, architect: Carlo Rossi

156 View of the Academic Room (Room 15)

They are characterised by their particular proximity and resemblance to man. This particular illustration gained its title from the thick golden locks of the angel. The icon painter portrays the radiant, transformed flesh of a creature that is free of sin and faults. His eyes are bright and his gaze fathomless, its mysterious expression indicating to the viewer that the archangel is listening to the voice of God.

St George is one of the most revered and well-loved of the saints in Russia. One of the most popular tales celebrating the miraculous strength of this man who lived in the 3rd century AD is that of "St George and the Dragon", which, like so many mythological and folk stories, tells of a heroic individual vanquishing a monster. This is one type of icongraphic image in which the idea of St George attaining his might by virtue of his faith is particularly apparent. Against a scarlet background (the "colour of eternity"), a youthful, beardless rider gallops on a white horse. In his right hand he holds a lance with which he pierces the evil snake. The young man's visage expresses peace and radiant hope. Worship of St George became an integral part of early Russian culture and numerous monasteries and churches were erected in his honour. The image of the saint was first incorporated into the coat of arms of Moscow and later became a symbol of the entire early Russian state.

157 Russian Museum
Icon: *The Archangel Gabriel*
(*The Angel with the Golden Hair*)
12th century

158 Russian Museum
Icon: *St George and the Dragon*
15th century

An entire series of splendid large-scale portraits by Karl Briullov,
otherwise known as "the great Karl", hangs in the Russian Museum.
Gogol once wrote that, "his works are perhaps the first to be accessible
to everyone with their liveliness and pure mirror images of nature.
His works are the first that even an artist with a highly developed sense
of taste but no knowledge of art can understand (yet not all alike).
They are the first to have the enviable fate of enjoying world-wide
acclaim, and the most highly reputed of these to this day is "The Last
Day of Pompeii", which because of its unusual breadth and embrace
of all things beautiful, may perhaps be compared to an opera,
if only for the fact that opera is the conjunction of the threefold world
of art: painting, poetry and music. Briullov's paintings may
be called complete, universal creations. They combine all things".

159 Karl Briullov. 1799–1852
The Last Day of Pompeii. 1833

160 Karl Briullov. 1799–1852
Portrait of the Shishmarev Sisters. 1839

161 Ilya Repin. 1844–1930
The Zaporozhye Cossacks. 1880–1891

162 Vasily Surikov. 1848–1916
Taking of a Snow Fortress. 1891

163 Ivan Shishkin. 1832–1898
Mast-Tree Grove. 1898

164 Ivan Aivazovsky. 1817–1900
The Tenth Wave. 1850

The Russian Museum owns the world's best collection of works by the Russian avant-garde artists, including such internationally acclaimed painters as Wassily Kandinsky, Kasimir Malevich and Pavel Filonov. Kandinsky was the founder of abstract painting, the first to find new ways of expressing the spiritual side of human existence and of liberating art from the study of objects by exploring the vibrancy and expressiveness of colour and rhythm. The Petersburg artist Filonov developed his own technique of "analytical art".

165 Nikolai Roerich. 1874–1947
Guests from Overseas. 1902

166 Mikhail Vrubel. 1856–1910
Demon in Flight. 1899

167 Nathan Altman. 1889–1970
Portrait of Anna Akhmatova. 1914

The architectural centrepiece of the square was the Mikhailovsky Palace (1819–1825), named after its owner, Grand Duke Mikhail Pavlovich, the younger brother of Alexander I and Nicholas II. Rossi incorporated two different designs into the exterior of the building. The main façade, which faces the square, was given a formal appearance. At the centre of the composition is an eight-column portico, mounted on a ground floor arcade. A splendid frieze consisting of 44 bas-reliefs (sculptor: Vasily Demut-Malinovsky) serves not only as an element of the décor, but also as a reminder to the Russian population of the victory gained in the war of 1812.

The design of the palace façade that overlooks the Mikhailovsky Garden emphasises the link with the natural landscape. On the ground floor, an open terrace with a flight of steps forms the exit into the park. On the Moika Embankment, where the wooden palace of Catherine II stood during the Petrine era, Rossi erected a pavilion and landing stage, whose elegant

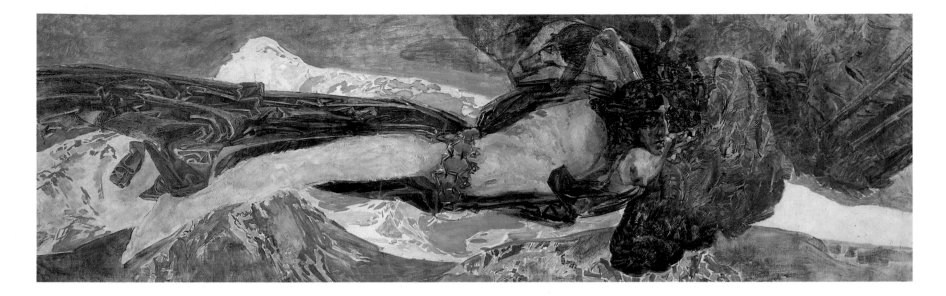

His works organically combine
the objective and the subjective,
the rational and the intuitive.
The objective world, when
subjected to the analysis of the
brush, is transformed into
a picture of the universal, of that
which is conceived by the energy
of the Creator. Malevich, having
studied Impressionism and
Cubism, completed the transi-
tion to formlessness by "invent-
ing" Suprematism – a variety
of geometric abstraction.
Suprematism, in the artist's own
words, can be divided into three
stages represented by an equal
number of squares, black,
red and white. "The basis for
their construction was an
essential economical principle,
i.e., to convey the power of statics
or of visible, dynamic peace
in one dimension."

→

168   Kasimir Malevich. 1878–1935
Red Cavalry. 1918

169   Wassily Kandinsky. 1866–1944
Composition No. 223. 1919

170   Wassily Kandinsky. 1866–1944
Twilight. 1917

171   Kasimir Malevich. 1878–1935
Portrait of a Woman. c. 1930

172   Liubov Popova. 1889–1924
Man+Air+Space

173   Kasimir Malevich. 1878–1935
Suprematism. 1915–1916

174   Alexandra Ekster. 1882–1949
Constructive Still Life. 1917

175 North façade of the Mikhailovsky Palace (Russian Museum)

176 Portico of the Russian Museum

proportions and beautiful details make it a delightful adornment to the riverbank. The remaining buildings situated on the square itself were erected over the course of the following century. For all of the architects working on the designs of these buildings, the unofficial point of reference was the Empire style, traits of which were so beautifully incorporated into the works of Carlo Rossi. An example of such an approach to design is the building that houses the Museum of Russian Ethnography (1911, architect: Vasily Svinin).

Arts Square is a monument to the Pushkin era, the "Golden Age" of Russian culture. Hence, a statue of Pushkin was erected in the centre of the square in 1957, the work of the famous and talented sculptor Mikhail Anikushin.

177 Yeliseev's shop. 1902–1903,
architect: Gavriil Baranovsky

On the Griboedov Canal side, the west wing of the Russian Museum adjoins the Mikhailovsky Palace. This is the so-called Benois Wing, built in the same Classical style as the rest of the palace (architects: Leonty Benois and Serguei Ovsianikov). Although construction did not start until 1914, first the onset of war and then the events of the Revolution delayed the process, which was completed significantly later. Its designers envisaged the Benois Wing as a place for special displays by various collectives and unions of artists that did not have their own exhibition rooms. This two-storey building provides a beautiful complement to the unique ensemble created by Carlo Rossi.

Besides Gostiny Dvor, there is another no less famous emporium on Nevsky Prospekt, at the junction with Malaya Sadovaya Street. This belonged to one of the representatives of a famous dynasty of merchants, Grigory Yeliseev. In the 18th century, this spot was occupied by a building that had undergone several renovations, namely the home of one of Empress Elizabeth's favourites, Alexei Razumovsky. Today, the building that houses the Yeliseev's shop is also the home of the Akimov Comedy Theatre.

This Art Nouveau style edifice was built in 1903 to designs by the architect Gavriil Baranovsky, but no trade was conducted here until the following year once the costly decorations had been completed. The new building provoked a storm of criticism from local aesthetes and people who were intent on maintaining the integrity of the city's historical appearance. The building, made entirely of stone and metal, is decorated on the outside with sculptural figures, amongst which Mercury, the patron of trade, is immediately recognisable. The huge window in the Nevsky façade, framed by the stone walls, is truly striking. The ground floor is occupied by a vast shop floor, embellished with unusually lavish ornaments and adorned with splendid light fittings. From the very outset, the plans of the premises included space for auditoriums, which were intended for hire. Yeliseev had noted the desperate need for theatre and concert halls at the time, particularly in the city centre. He was not mistaken in his venture, which soon began to generate considerable income.

178   Yeliseev' shop. Interior

179   Architect Rossi Street

159

The entire architectural ensemble of Ostrovsky Square, which opens out onto Nevsky Prospekt, and the street that links it to another smaller plaza now known as Lomonosov Square, became one of Rossi's greatest masterpieces of urban design. The humble task of building the Alexandrinsky Theatre evolved into a fantastic plan to create an entire block.

To begin with, two small pavilions (1817–1818), linked by a beautiful fence, appeared on the eastern side of the square. They served as the arsenal of the Anichkov Palace (1741–1750s), a building that a number of architects had a hand in, including Rastrelli.

The palace was built for Elizabeth Petrovna, who presented it to her favourite and, as legend has it, morganatic husband, Count Alexei Razumovsky. The building, which stood at the entrance to the city in the 18th century, is surrounded by a large park and overlooks the Fontanka River and the Anichkov Bridge. Before the October Revolution 1917, it was the site of one of the imperial residences.

180   Monument to Catherine II. 1873, designed
by Mikhail Mikeshin, sculptors:
Alexander Opekushin, Matvei Chizhov

181   Apollo's chariot on the pediment
of the Alexandrinksy Theatre

182   Alexandrinsky Theatre. 1828–1832,
architect: Carlo Rossi

183–185 Monument to Catherine II. Details

БЕЦКОЙ

КН. ПОТЕМКИНЪ   КН. СУВОРОВЪ

The main component of the Ostrovsky Square ensemble, the Alexandrinsky Theatre, was erected in 1832, and is now an outstanding monument to Russian Classicism. The upper half of the building's main façade is decorated with a colonnade of six columns. Atop the attic stands the chariot of Apollo, the leader of the Muses, while the very attic itself is decorated with the image of Glory. The solid, well-proportioned building of the theatre was once clearly visible from Nevsky Prospekt. Today, however, the trees that have grown up on the square obscure the view and distort our perception of the broad sweep of the square. Behind the theatre is one of the most perfect streets in St Petersburg, bearing the name of Carlo Rossi.

In 1873, a monument to Catherine II was erected in the centre of the square (design: Mikhail Mikeshin, sculptors: Alexander Opekushin and Matvei Chizhov). At the feet of the towering Empress sit eminent figures of her time, including dignitaries, military leaders, scientists and artists.

Built at Peter I's behest in 1715 on the main road that joined the capital with the outlying villages, the Anichkov Bridge was one of the first bridges in Petersburg. Over the years, the appearance of the Anichkov Bridge has changed several times in accordance with the type of building materials used. In 1841, it finally acquired the appearance it has today. It was rebuilt in stone in just six months, a record-breaking achievement at the time. The principal feature of the bridge is the sculptural ensemble known as 'The Taming of the Horse'. It was Klodt too who suggested that the statues be placed on the Anichkov Bridge. Only two components of the original bronze sculptural group (1841) were installed: the remaining figures, facing Liteiny Prospekt, were substituted with painted plaster models since, by order of Nicholas I, the bronze originals were sent to Berlin as a gift for the king of Prussia. When the sculptor cast a second set in bronze, these too were sent abroad, this time to Naples. Later, in 1848, once the plaster statues had been destroyed by the vagaries of the Petersburg climate, Klodt created two new groups, different to their predecessors, for the vacant pedestals on the bridge. The bronze suite on the Anichkov Bridge continues to occupy an important place amongst the sculptural embellishments of Petersburg.

←

186   Eagle. Railings of the square in front of the Anichkov Palace

←

187   Rossi Pavilion. 1817–1818, architect: Carlo Rossi

188   Anichkov Bridge. Sculptural group: *The Taming of the Horse* 1841–1850, sculptor: Piotr Klodt

189   Anichkov Bridge. 1841, architect: Alexander Briullov

190   Anichkov Bridge. Sculptural group: *The Taming of the Horse* 1846–1850, sculptor: Piotr Klodt

On the corner of Nevsky and the Fontanka stands the Beloselsky-Belozersky Palace, which was fundamentally redesigned by Andrei Stackenschneider in 1847–1848 "in the style of Rastrelli" with the Stroganov Palace serving as an unusual blueprint. The palace's first owner was Prince Alexander Beloselsky-Belozersky, a member of a family line leading back to the Kievan princes and the princes of Beloselsk, who earned a name for themselves in the service of Peter I. This dignitary, who lived at the time of Catherine the Great, was extremely well educated and collected works of art. The prince's passion for collecting was inherited by his descendants, and they succeeded in amassing an enviable collection of artworks during the time that they inhabited the palace. In 1884, financial difficulties compelled the Beloselsky-Belozersky princes to sell the "family nest" to Grand Duke Sergei Alexandrovich. The palace's last owner was Grand Duke Dmitry Pavlovich, Sergei Alexandrovich's nephew. He owes his place in the annals of history to his part in the murder of Grigory Rasputin, after which Dmitry was regarded by many as a national hero. After the Revolution, he resurfaced in France, where he met Coco Chanel and even became her lover for a time. Dmitry died in 1942 in Davos.

191 Beloselsky-Belozersky Palace
1847–1848, architect:
Andrei Stackenschneider

192 Beloselsky-Belozersky Palace
Gold Drawing Room
→
193 Grand Princess Elizabeth
Fedorovna. Photograph

194 Beloselsky-Belozersky Palace
Oak Room

195 Beloselsky-Belozersky Palace
Main Staircase

196 Beloselsky-Belozersky Palace
View from the window of the Gold
Drawing Room

Grand Duke Sergei Alexandrovich, Alexander II's fifth son, acquired the palace in view of his impending marriage to Elizabeth Fedorovna, the elder sister of Nicholas II's bride-to-be. Everyone who knew this woman loved and admired her. "A rare beauty, brilliant mind, subtle humour, saintly patience and noble heart – such were the virtues of this surprising woman." Yet she did not enjoy married life with the Grand Duke, a rough, suspicious and rather cruel man, although she tried painstakingly to hide it. Her life ended tragically in 1918 when, together with several other members of the imperial family, she was thrown alive into a mineshaft near the city of Alapaevsk in the Urals.

Today, the Beloselsky-Belozersky Palace is the home of the City Cultural Centre. This organisation strives to preserve the artistic atmosphere that once prevailed within the building's walls.

The palaces of Petersburg often look out over the water. A particularly large number of these are to be found on the banks of the Fontanka River. As a rule, in the 18th century, these were a part of the large estates and gardens that overlooked either Sadovaya Street or Liteiny Prospekt. An excellent example of these is the "Fountain House", the home of the Sheremetev family (1746–1750) designed by Savva Chevakinsky and the Sheremetevs' serf architect, Fedor Argunov. In 1867, the architect Nikolai Benois separated the main courtyard from the embankment with wrought iron railings and gates into which he skilfully incorporated Baroque motifs. Certain inhabitants of the Fountain House have left a lasting mark on the history of Russian culture. In the early 20th century, Poetry herself took up residence in the guise of Anna Akhmatova.

197 Sheremetev family coat of arms on the gateway

198 Sheremetev Palace. 1746–1750, architects: Savva Chevakinsky, Fedor Argunov

199 Shuvalov Palace. 1844–1846, architects: Bernard Simon, Nikolai Efimov

200 Shuvalov Palace Main Staircase

201 Shuvalov Palace Blue Drawing Room

→

202 Fontanka River Embankment

203 Fontanka River Embankment Trinity (Izmailovsky) Cathedral

A little further down on the right-hand bank of the Fontanka stands the palace of the Naryshkin-Shuvalov family. In 1799, the residence became the property of a member of the ancient Russian line of the Naryshkins, Dmitry Lvovich. His wife was a woman of amazing beauty and even the crown prince, Alexander I, could not withstand her charms. The two fell in love and had children, of whom the younger girl, Sofia, was her father's favourite. Her premature death in 1824 affected Alexander very deeply: "She is dead. I am punished for all my sins."

In 1844, work began on the remodelling of the palace in accordance with plans by the architect Bernard Simon. Today, visitors to this former residence are enchanted by the fruits of his fertile imagination that festoon the interiors.

In 1964, the building became the home of the International House of Friendship.

Within the space of just one hundred years, St Petersburg had evolved into the seemly embodiment of a major European city and state capital. The many colonnades adorning its buildings earned it the title of "Northern Palmira", while its numerous bridges, rivers and canals caused it to be deemed the "Northern Venice". Such comparisons reveal the desire of past generations of Petersburgers to emphasise the city's importance and extol its beauty. It goes without saying that Petersburg is not simply a city of the 18th and 19th centuries, although it is precisely these eras that shaped the inimitable appearance of the northern capital.

In the second half of the 18th century, during the reign of Paul I, a military parade ground known as the Field of Mars was founded on Poteshny Meadow, once the site of public fetes, splendid firework displays and a large public theatre. The Field of Mars stretched for 500 metres from north to south and 300 metres from east to west. It was a huge open space that was snow-covered in winter and dusty in the summer, hence its nickname the "Petersburg Sahara". Along the western edge of the field ran the barracks of the Light Guards of the Pavlovsk Regiment, who earned considerable recognition in the war of 1812. The barracks were built in 1818 according to designs by Vasily Stasov on the site of the palace in which Elizabeth Petrovna had lived prior to her ascension to the throne. The regular Classical façade of the barracks also extends the length of the three neighbouring buildings. The barrenness of the square is softened by the greenery of the nearby Summer Garden and Mikhailovsky Gardens. The square on the Field of Mars itself came into being in 1924 after participants in the February Revolution of 1917 were buried there and a monument (the work of the architect Lev Rudnev) was erected over the graves. Blank verses by the people's commissar for education, Anatoly Lunacharsky, are carved on the face of the stone slabs of the Monument to the Victims of the February Revolution 1917. In the 1930s, grass was sown on the Field of Mars and the place was transformed into a park.

AROUND THE FIELD OF
MARS AND THE CHURCH
ON THE SPILLED BLOOD

204 Panoramic view
of St Petersburg from the roof
of the Mikhailovsky Castle

176

The Field of Mars is separated from the Neva by Suvorov Square, named after Generalissimo Prince Alexander Suvorov, who is commemorated by a statue by Mikhail Kozlovsky (1801). When work first began on the statue by order of Paul I, it was intended for a different spot, namely the square in front of the Mikhailovsky Castle. However, Suvorov, a highly independent character, soon fell out of favour with the capricious Emperor, and the monument was thus installed on the Field of Mars. Although it initially stood at the northernmost edge of the field, it was later moved to the centre of the square. The great Russian military leader is shown in knightly armour in the semblance of Mars, the god of war. Suvorov has found a permanent place in the nation's memory with the help of his grateful descendants, who had a special museum built (1900s, architects: Alexander von Gogen and Herman Grimm) in which everything related to the commander's life and military accomplishments is preserved. Suvorov Square is the last in a series of squares that look out over the left bank of the Neva. The wide green expanse, together with the Summer Garden, is a final view of old Petersburg, a city in which the architecture "in formidable nakedness resounds imperiously with the stone tongue of genius".

205 View of the Field of Mars from
the roof of the Mikhailovsky Castle

In the 1830s, the Neo-Russian style emerged in Russia, an attempt to return to the Orthodox traditions of church architecture. Until recently, a negative opinion has been held of this interesting phenomenon in Russian culture due to the critical attitude of art historians at the turn of the twentieth century. Many of the buildings were ruthlessly destroyed and those that remained, no longer put to their original use or bearing their original appearance, quietly awaited their demise. It is thus all the more gratifying that specialists have now turned their attention to these buildings and rehabilitated them in the eyes of both the public and the local authorities. As a result, the Church on the Spilled Blood has finally regained its good name and striking appearance.

"The Church of the Resurrection of Christ on the Site of the Mortal Wounding of Emperor Alexander II" (such is the cathedral's canonical title) was built on the spot where the Emperor was assassinated on 1 March 1881 by Grinevitsky, a member of the "Narodnaya volya" group. Hence its commonly accepted and better known name, "The Church on the Spilled Blood", and the prejudice borne it by the Soviet authorities. In 1970, this incredible building, now a milestone in the history of church restoration, became a part of the St Isaac's Cathedral museum network.

206 Church on the Spilled Blood
(Church of the Resurrection)
1883–1907, architects: Alfred Parland,
Archimandrite Ignaty (Ignaty Malyshev)

207 Cupolas of the Church
on the Spilled Blood

The erection of churches in honour of memorable events is a long-standing tradition that dates back to the days of early Russian architecture, thus the suggestion to build a church in 1881 was immediately approved by the St Petersburg City Council. The original plans were rejected by Alexander III who wanted the church to be "built in the purely Russian style of the 17th century". He approved the designs submitted by the architect Alfred Parland and Archimandrite Ignaty (Ignaty Malyshev). It was Father Ignaty who proposed the name of the cathedral and the basic design of the building in the form of the five open petals of an immortelle. Parland decided to use features in his decorative designs that were reminiscent of St Basil's Cathedral in Moscow, which was regarded as a unique symbol of the "national character" in Russian architecture at the time.

The construction of the church and work on the decor took 24 years (1883–1907). The church is 81 metres high with a total area of 1,642.35 square metres. Stonecutters, artists, mosaicists, ceramists and enamellers were involved in the creation of its striking artistic ornaments. The outside of the church is decorated largely with mosaics, while the cupolas are covered with bright enamels and the hipped roofs with coloured tiles.

The 308 mosaics, with a total area of 6,560 square metres, are a true artistic and cultural treasure. Together they make up a unique collection, which has no equal anywhere else in the world. Besides traditional iconographic subjects, the coats of arms of Russian cities and administrative units are also depicted in the mosaics that cover three sides of the bell-tower. The mosaics were prepared by both Russian experts and a number of foreign firms.

Sketches for the mosaics were made by a group of over 25 artists. Of these men, we can single out Viktor Vasnetsov, who created two of the images for the interior, *The Saviour* and *The Mother and Child*, and Mikhail Nesterov, who worked on the depictions of *The Holy Saviour* and *The Resurrection* on the façades as well as a number of mosaics inside the church. Forty-two of the mosaics are the work of Nikolai Kharlamov, including *The Pantocrator* on the plafond of the central dome, which is one of the artist's most memorable works. *The Eucharist* (artist: Nikolai Kharlamov) is a liturgical interpretation of the Last Supper, depicting the sacred idea of the establishment of the rite of Communion, rather than an historical portrayal showing Christ's prediction of His imminent betrayal by Judas. In *The Eucharist*, the Saviour offers His disciples the holy bread with His right hand ("Take, this is my body"), while with His left He gives them the cup of wine

("This is my blood of the covenant, which is poured out for many"). The contributions made by Andrei Riabushkin and Vasily Beliaev to the mosaic designs are also worthy of note.

The Church on the Spilled Blood in St Petersburg aroused particularly strong feelings. "People came here specially to admire the unusual décor, and when they bought a candle, they were given, by way of a memento, a small piece of the smalt from which the mosaics decorating the church were composed" (Nina Kuteinikova).

Although the love of the faithful did not save the church from being closed in 1930, the will of God saved it from destruction during the Blockade when a shell fell on a cupola but did not explode. The building was further preserved by the bravery of the sappers who, under the leadership of Viktor Demidov, risked their lives in 1961 to defuse the missile. The skill, expertise

209 Church on the Spilled Blood
Mosaic: *The Crucifixion*
Designed by Alfred Parland

210 View of Griboedov Canal
and the Church on the Spilled Blood

The Church on the Spilled Blood is both an historical monument and a work of art. The men who built it were given the difficult task of incorporating the spot on which the terrible crime was committed into the interior of the church. The site of the murder is marked by a special chapel in the western part of the building beneath the bell. Here, in an area slightly below floor-level, part of the carriageway and railings that were stained with blood at the time of the assassination can be seen.

The specific conditions for the construction of the church are the reason for another of the building's idiosyncrasies: it has no central entrance. Instead, on either side of the bell-tower is a parvis with its own doorway. Inside the Church on the Spilled Blood there is not a single painting: the walls are almost entirely covered with mosaics.

211 Church on the Spilled Blood
Main altar. Mosaic: *The Eucharist*
Designed by Nikolai Kharlamov

→
212 Church on the Spilled Blood
Cupola. Mosaic: *The Pantocrator*
Designed by Nikolai Kharlamov

213 Church on the Spilled Blood
Northern icon-case
Mosaic: *St Alexander Nevsky*
Designed by Mikhail Nesterov

214 Church on the Spilled Blood
Mosaic: *Raising of a Widow's Son
in Nain*. Designed by Valerian Otmar

215 Church on the Spilled Blood
Mosaic: *Christ in the House
of Simon the Pharisee.*
Designed by Firs Zhuravlev

216 Church on the Spilled Blood
Interior

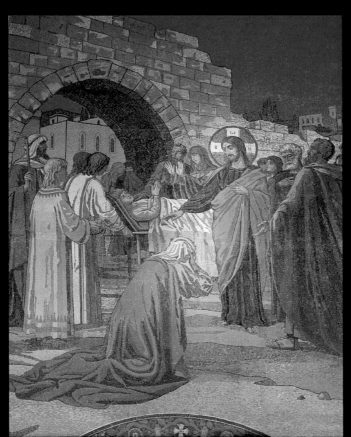

217 Church on the Spilled Blood
South façade

218 Egor Botman. ?–1891
Portrait of Alexander II. 1856

219 Railings of the Mikhailovsky
Garden alongside the Church
on the Spilled Blood

and truly selfless efforts of the restorers, engineers, architects, technicians and everyone who worked on the restoration of the church have made it possible for this wonderful and unique edifice to once more bask in its own splendour and delight and amaze all who see it.

Mikhailovsky Castle was built on the site of the wooden Summer Palace of Elizabeth Petrovna in the Summer Garden. The latter building and surrounding area of land was destroyed at the behest of Paul I, the man who commissioned the construction of the castle (1784–1800, architects: Vasily Bazhenov and Vincenzo Brenna). By design, the building constitutes a square with an octagonal courtyard in the middle. The main façade faces southeast and is characterised by a riot of ornamentation. In the centre is the main entrance to the inner courtyard.

The castle served as the imperial residence for only 40 days. In 1823, it was taken over by the Engineering Academy and acquired its second name, the "Engineer's Castle". From 1837 to 1842, Fedor Dostoevsky was educated here. One of the most "Petersburg" writers, he disliked the city and its founder intensely and refused to acknowledge "Peter's doings" as the Europeanisation of Russia.

Peter I created something more than just a city or even a capital at the mouth of the Neva. He set out to establish an earthly Paradise, which in recent years had begun to be depicted in the form of the garden. The oldest garden in Petersburg, the oldest "Paradise" on the banks of the Neva, is the Summer Garden, which is one of the most magnificent and unique monuments to 18th century park culture.

The garden was laid at the source of the Nameless Channel (now known as the Fontanka) almost concurrently with the founding of Petersburg in 1704. From plans dating from 1716 it is apparent that the garden occupied the ground between the Neva and the Moika, and the Fontanka and the Swan Moat, i.e., precisely the same area that it covers today.

The scope of Peter's plans for the Summer Garden was enormous. Initially, the garden stretched from the Neva to what would eventually become Nevsky Prospekt. Gradually, however, the city expanded and the value of land in the city centre increased, thus gardens and

220 Panoramic view of St Petersburg from the roof of the Mikhailovsky Castle

The castle was named after the church within its walls, which was dedicated to the Archangel Michael, the dread leader of the heavenly host. The building's appearance is a reflection of its owner's darkly romantic imagination. The castle was surrounded by a moat, which was passable only by means of drawbridges. Each of the faces of the building differs in its design. The façade overlooking the Moika and the Summer Garden boasts a first-floor open terrace and a magnificent flight of steps decorated with statues of Hercules and Flora. Behind the windows of the first floor lies the room in which Paul I was assassinated on 11 March 1801, in spite of the thick defensive walls of the building and the presence of the tsar's personal armed guard.

In front of the castle, on the parade ground, stands a monument to Peter the Victor, the work of Carlo-Bartolomeo Rastrelli, father of the renowned architect. In its day, the model for this sculpture was approved by Peter the Great himself, yet the path to the realisation of the sculptor's plans and the raising of the monument was a long one. It was not until 1800, under Paul I, that the statue finally assumed its place, as evidenced by the inscription on the pedestal: "To great-grandfather from great-grandson."

221 Mikhailovsky Castle
South façade

222 Mikhailovsky Castle. 1784–1800, architects: Vasily Bazhenov, Vincenzo Brenna

Paul I (1754–1801) reigned from 1796 to 1801. "Highly-strung and impressionable by nature, Paul endured a difficult school of life, which made him irritable and suspicious of others. He witnessed the over-throw of his father, knew of the events surrounding his mother's ascension to the throne, and throughout her entire reign he felt that he was in disgrace" (Grand Duke Nikolai Romanov). Having come to power quite late in life at the age of 42, Paul I began to implement changes with particular energy and bitterness, creating a strict regime within the state, although many of his undertakings were undoubtedly of a positive nature. Members of the nobility were greatly upset by the decrees that restricted their civil and personal liberty, and the ranks of dissatisfied individuals grew with the introduction of reforms to the army. All of this led to the burgeoning of a plot within the highest social circles, which was headed by Count Piotr von der Pahlen, one of the tsar's closest confidants. On the night of 11 March 1801, Paul I was suffocated by a group of conspir-ators with the secret approval of his own son, the future Emperor Alexander. Other members of the tsar's family had also been aware of the impending attempt on his life.

223   Mikhailovsky Castle. Church of the Archangel Michael. Iconostasis

224   Salvatore Tonci. 1756–1844
Portrait of Paul I

→
225   View of Mikhailovsky Castle beyond the ornamental lake in the Summer Garden

allotments began to give way to buildings. The garden also dwindled until it assumed the dimensions shown in the 1716 plan of the city.

Both Russian and foreign architects took part in the creation of the Summer Garden. It was envisaged as a "regular garden" of the Baroque era. In the time of Peter the Great, such gardens were referred to as "Dutch" gardens because the Emperor had become familiar with the style while he was in Holland. In the history of landscape gardening they are described as "French" gardens, since the grounds of the Palace of Versailles belonging to Louis XIV served as the model for such gardens in Europe. They are characterised by straight avenues, thick curtains of bushes and trees cut into geometric shapes, and copses or rather natural, open-air rooms. Amidst the thick greenery, the groves and narrow pathways formed labyrinths and secluded corners.

The French parks had a certain significance. These were the gardens of the age of Newton, the discoverer of quantum mechanics, and the rational philosophers, Descartes and Leibnitz. Here, nature was ennobled by the intellect and reduced to mathematical formulae, while the endless vistas of the avenues reflected European culture's striving for continual progress.

Such gardens were embellished with images of gods from the Greco-Roman pantheon, which had recently ceased to be the symbols of a generation of heathens and had come to be considered as formulae for the expression of abstract notions. Thus, Venus stood for Love and Beauty, Minerva for Wisdom and Knowledge, Hercules for Strength and Might, etc. The artist was also free to invent visual images to give concrete expression to elusive concepts.

In Peter's day, only one genuine antique sculpture stood in the Summer Garden, a statue of Venus, which can now be seen in the Hermitage. At the time, it was watched over by an armed guard, since the open display of a naked female form was akin to the coming of the Whore of Babylon in the eyes of the Russian Orthodox public.

The remaining statues in the Summer Garden (there were 220, of which 91 have survived) were, for the most part, created by Italian sculptors at the beginning of the 18th century.

226 Railings around the Summer Garden. 1771–1784,
architect: Yuri Velten, Piotr Egorov

→
227 Summer Garden. Statue of Ceres. Late 17th century
Sculptor T. Quellinius

228 Summer Garden. Central avenue

229 Summer Garden
Decorative sculpture. 18th – early 19th century

In those days, there were workshops in Rome and Venice that practically mass-produced such garden ornaments. Thus the statue of Apollo – an exact copy of the Apollo Belvedere – and the Muse of dance, Terpsichore, originated from the famous workshop of Gropelli. An entire set of the Muses was created for the Summer Garden, but only three remain today. Sets of allegorical statues were also commissioned, including the seasons, the virtues, the sciences and others.

Amongst the attractions of the Summer Garden were numerous fountains from which the Unnamed Channel gained the name "Fontanka". A complex hydraulic device was developed to operate them, but was totally destroyed by a terrible flood in 1777. The 18th century pavilions also failed to survive. Built at the beginning of the 18th century, the "gallery

on marble pillars with a marble floor" was replaced by a magnificent wrought iron fence (designed by Yury Felten) with columns hewn from Finnish granite. The "best grille in the world" was erected along the northern edge of the garden, separating it from the thoroughfare along the Palace Embankment. The railings were created over a period of 15 years, right up until 1784.

One of the sights of the Summer Garden is the monument to the famous Russian fabulist, Ivan Krylov, whose translations of the tales of La Fontaine as well as his own works are enjoyed by readers to this day. The statue, the most modern of

the sculptural works to be found in the Summer Garden, was unveiled on 12 May 1855.

The idea behind the composition was totally unprecedented in mid-19th century monumental sculpture. Its creator, Piotr Klodt, departed from the traditional stylised interpretation of his subject and depicted the famous writer in a natural light, resting in the shade of the trees of the Summer Garden. The figure's "majestic stillness" is the only thing it has in common with the Classical heroes of monumental sculpture. Klodt knew Krylov well and thus took pains to give an accurate rendering of the writer's physical features and

In 1711–1712, in the northeastern corner of the garden, Peter I's Summer Palace was built (architect: Andreas Schlüter, Domenico Trezzini), which, contrary to the traditions of park design, did not constitute the centrepiece of the composition, but was intended only for personal use by the tsar and his family. In accordance with the tastes of its owner, it resembles a Dutch house, and overlooks the Neva on one side and the Fontanka on another. It was possible to get to the house directly from the water, due to the creation of a small "harbour" or reservoir leading into the Fontanka. This modest house, a two-storey building with a high roof, hardly conforms to the idea of a palace fit for the "founder of the sovereign state". It is decorated simply with reliefs between the windows on the ground and first floor. It now preserves the memory of its owner, housing a museum, in which the interiors have been faithfully restored to show how the palace looked when it was first built.

230 Peter I's Summer Palace
1710–1712, architects: Andreas Schlüter,
Domenico Trezzini

231 Summer Palace
Peter I's Bedroom

232 Summer Palace. Peter I's Study

familiar pose. The statue's unusual pedestal, crowded with the heroes of Krylov's fables, is also worthy of note. The sculptor and animal painter rendered the fictional creatures with great skill, achieving a certain lifelikeness in their appearance. The famous Russian illustrator, Alexander Agin, was also involved in the creation of this work, producing entire series of sketches that were subsequently transformed into high relief.

Petersburg's main embankment, the Palace Embankment, owes its name to the magnificent edifices that, like the jewels of a necklace, adorn the left bank of the Neva. The architectural complex of the Hermitage Museum makes up half of the Palace Embankment ensemble. The remaining stretch of the embankment is lined with palaces that once belonged, for the most part, to members of the royal family. The earliest of the grand-ducal buildings on the Palace Embankment is the Marble Palace (1768–1785, architect: Antonio Rinaldi).

233 Summer Garden. Monument to Ivan Krylov
1855, sculptor: Piotr Klodt

234, 235 Monument to Ivan Krylov
Details of the bas-reliefs

236 Summer Garden. Main gate

On the banks of the Fontanka stand educational institutions as well as palaces. Opposite the Summer Garden is a building that was developed from an 18th century residence in the 1830s by the architect Vasily Stasov. Until the Revolution, it was the home of the School of Jurisprudence, which trained young men to become functionaries for legal departments. The first 14 students graduated in 1840. Amongst these men were the composers Alexander Serov (father of the Russian artist, Valentin Serov) and Piotr Ilyich Tchaikovsky, the poet Alexei Apukhtin and the art critic Vladimir Stasov.

Nearby, on the street that runs parallel to the Fontanka, stands the Mukhina Industrial Arts Academy (formerly the College of Draughtsmanship).

The college once bore the name of Baron Ludwig Stieglitz, a rich banker who donated part of his enormous fortune to the building.

The college itself was erected by the architects Alexander Krakau and Robert Hedike between 1879–1881, while the college museum was constructed by the architect Maximilian Messmacher between 1885–1895.

237 Railings of the Summer Garden in winter

238 Terrace of the Summer Garden Swan Moat

239 Summer Garden Detail of the railings

→
240 View of the Palace Embankment

The only residence not to be named after its owner, it is a unique monument to decorative art. The façade of the first and second floors of the palace are clad in marble of various shades from all over the world. The palace interiors were also decorated with marble, but only the main staircase and the lower tier of the large hall have survived. Although the marble has faded and lost its brilliance due to the local climate, the palace is rightfully regarded as a gem of early Russian Classical architecture. The palace was first owned by Grigory Orlov, a favourite of Catherine II who presented him with this token of her "gratitude".

After Orlov's death in 1783, long before the building was completed, Catherine bought it back from his successors and gave it to her grandson, Konstantin Pavlovich. From that

241 Marble Palace. 1768–1785, architect: Antonio Rinaldi, sculptor Fedot Shubin

242 Marble Palace. Marble Hall

243 Stefano Torelli. 1712–1780
Portrait of Grigori Orlov. Not earlier than 1763

The original owner of the palace, Grand Duke Vladimir(the son of Alexander II) is known primarily for the fact that as of 1876, for a period of 34 years, he was president of the Academy of Arts. Of particular note are the beautifully preserved, lavish interiors, of which the most striking is the main staircase in the French Renaissance style. It is decorated with paintings, sculptures and stuccowork. Moreover, many of the rooms are hung with paintings. One of the first canvases to be brought to the new palace was Repin's "Barge-Haulers on the Volga". The owner's real pride and joy, however, was his extensive collection of antique weapons.

After the Revolution, the only thing that saved the palace's interiors and its well-stocked library from ruin was the fact that it was taken over by the Committee for the Improvement of the Lives of Academics, hence its name the "Academicians House".

244 Palace of Grand Duke Vladimir (Academicians House). 1867–1872, architect: Alexander Rezanov

245 Palace of Grand Duke Vladimir Main Staircase

246 Palace of Grand Duke Vladimir Red Drawing Room

moment until 18 May 1918, the building served as the residence first of the Grand Duke, then of one of his six children, Konstantin Konstantinovich, who in turn had six sons and two daughters. Konstantin Konstantinovich combined his military career with the study of music, theatre and literature. Seventy of his verses, which he signed with the initials *K. R.*, have been set to music by Piotr Tchaikovsky, Serguei Rakhmaninov and other composers.

The palace now belongs to the Russian Museum. In the courtyard stands a statue of Alexander III astride a horse. This work by Paolo Trubetsky was located in the centre of the square near the Moscow Railway Station until 1936. When it was first erected, the monument aroused mixed reactions from the public. Many people saw it as a caricature of the Emperor, although the sculptor had allowed himself to be inspired by the Russian *bylinas* (heroic poems) while creating this image.

Today, the former grand-ducal palaces situated on the Palace Embankment are mainly occupied by academic institutions. Thus, the palace of Grand Duke Vladimir (1867–1872, architect: Alexander Rezanov), is now the Academicians House. The palace was finally completed in 1872. Like many of the residences in the district, it covers a significant area of land from the embankment to Millionnaya Street. The design of the building's main façade, which comprises Italian architectural motifs of the Renaissance era, is intended to impress. The ornaments on the exterior of the palace include 14 medallions bearing coats of arms. The grand portal is adorned with a carved oak tambour.

247 View of the Trinity Bridge and the Peter and Paul Fortress from the Kutuzov Embankment

By the mid-19th century, Palace Square had assumed the architectural form it has today. By contrast, the city's oldest square, created at the same time as the Peter and Paul Fortress, has retained nothing but its original boundaries. To begin with, this place, which was to become known as the "Trinity Square" on Petrograd Island, was shaped by the elements, but was soon turned into a square, named in honour of the wooden Trinity Church located there. At the same time, Peter's first wooden house was built along with homes for his retinue. Of all these buildings, only the imperial dwelling has survived. It remains standing to this day, protected by a special brick shell.

Peter chose the site for his first house in Petersburg himself. This small building, labelled the "Red Mansion", was built in just three days from 24 to 26 May 1703. It is the only wooden construction in the city that has survived to this day and remains standing on its original site. Its dimensions are small (12 x 5.5 x 5.72 metres), the outside walls are painted to look like bricks, and the roof is covered with shingles (small wooden boards intended to resemble tiles). There are three rooms inside in addition to the hallway: a study, dining room and bedroom. During his own lifetime, Peter I was concerned that the house be preserved for his successors in the "distant future", thus in 1723 he ordered the construction of a protective gallery. All of the subsequent Russian monarchs, beginning with Elizabeth Petrovna, took care of this historic relic in accordance with the will of the formidable autocrat. The building's protective shell, which has changed in appearance over the course of time, has faithfully served its purpose.

Over the course of two centuries, work was carried out to reinforce the bank of the Neva in the vicinity of the building, and a small garden was laid out around it and subsequently enclosed by iron railings in 1875.

At the far end of the embankment stands the Nakhimov Naval Academy (1910–1912, architect: Alexander Dmitriev,

248 *Shih-tzu* statues at a landing on the Petrovskaya Embankment 1903, engineer: Andrei Pshenitsky; 1907, architect: Leonty Benois

design: Alexander Benois, sculptor: V. Kuznetsov), once the Peter the Great City College, where young men who have chosen to dedicate their lives to maritime service are trained.

On the stretch of river in front of the building, the cruiser *Aurora* is permanently moored. The ship was first launched in 1904. Its design is based upon that of an ancient frigate, hence its masts. The *Aurora* is famous not only for the shot fired from its deck on 25 October 1917 (by the old calendar), which signalled the storming of the Winter Palace during the October Revolution 1917, but also for the part it played in the Russo-Japanese war in the Pacific Ocean in 1904–1905 and the battle of Tsushima Strait, which ended in tragedy for the Russian navy. It was later converted into a training ship, and at the start of the Siege of Leningrad its cannons protected the city from German forces. The ship has been a museum since 1948. The famous gun, the bell and the crew's quarters can be viewed, along with an exhibition on the history of the *Aurora*.

Towards the end of the 19th century, the Petrograd Side became particularly popular amongst the wealthy and influential. Thenceforth, the district's main thoroughfare,

249 Peter the Great's House seen from the Petrovskaya Embankment

250 Peter the Great's House May, 24–26 1703

The image of Kamenoostrovsky Prospekt was determined in the 1910s. It was at this time that retrospection became a dominant trend in architecture, emerging around the same time as Art Nouveau. The former entailed the rejection of all things modern in favour of an idealised view of the past. Unlike Art Nouveau, it did not break with bygone eras, but incorporated techniques derived from architecture of different styles and schools, particularly the Renaissance. The reproduction of certain early features in contemporary buildings of a considerably larger size made it necessary for architects to increase these details relative to the size of the building. As a result, the architecture of this era is characterised by excessive proportions and an air of pomposity and theatricality. In the façades of no. 77 Bolshoy Prospekt on the Petrograd Side (1913–1916, architect: Andrei Belogrud) motifs from the architecture of Andreo Palladio are apparent. The corners of the main façade overlooking Lev Tolstoy Square are accentuated by protruding towers decorated with balustrades.

251 Kshesinskaya Mansion
1904–1906, architect: Alexander von Gogen

252 Rosenstein's house
1913–1916, architect: Andrei Belogrud

253 Austria Square

254 Detail on the front of the former home of the merchant Brant
architect: Roman Melzer

Kamenoostrovsky Prospekt, was actively developed and became known as the "Elysian Fields of Petersburg". One of the first residences to appear in this area of town was that of Mathilda Kshesinskaya, a famous prima ballerina from the Imperial Theatres. She was Nicholas I's first love, and their relationship lasted for approximately three years. In 1900, Kshesinskaya became acquainted with Grand Duke Alexander Vladimirovich, and in 1902 she bore him a son by the name of Vladimir. In 1904, Kshesinskaya bought a plot of land, and within two years the house and all its interiors were complete.

The mansion, designed by Alexander von Gogen, served both as a private residence and a venue for the various receptions and parties held by the celebrated ballerina. Kshesinskaya herself played an active part in designing the building, suggesting the layout of the rooms, the construction of a winter garden, and the décor of the apartments. The architectural complex of the palace included an angular gazebo overlooking the junction between two streets.

Mathilda Kshesinkskaya's house is a splendid example of the emergence of Art Nouveau in Petersburg architecture, characterised by asymmetrical designs, organically linked spaces, a range of components of varying sizes that combine to create an integral whole, and the use of stylised natural motifs.

The history of the building is as full of tragic events as the life of its owner. By a cruel twist of fate, the residence, which had once thrown its doors open to the very Emperor and many members of the royal family, became the site of the Bolshevik headquarters in 1917. Twenty years later, it became the Kirov Museum, and in 1957 it was turned into the Museum of the Revolution, renamed the "State Museum of Russian Political History" in 1991. Much of the building has since been restored and has resumed its original appearance. The monument to the residence's original owner, Mathilda Kshesinskaya, has been reinstalled, and the museum now contains an exhibit dedicated to her.

255 Convent of St John of Kronstadt Main building. 1900–1908, architect: Nikolai Nikonov

256 Convent of St John of Kronstadt Icon: *St John of Kronstadt*

257 Convent of St John of Kronstadt Interior of the Upper Church in the name of the Twelve Apostles

258 Convent of St John of Kronstadt. St John of Kronstadt's burial-vault

The Convent of St John of Kronstadt on the Karpovka River serves as a reminder of the saint who appeared in Petersburg in the second half of the 19th century and established this very institution. It is here too that John of Kronstadt is buried. The building was designed in the Byzantine style by Nikolai Nikonov (1900–1908). Although the convent was closed in 1923, it has since resumed its former function.

After graduating from theological college, John of Kronstadt (Ioann Sergiev, 1829–1908) spent 53 years as the archpriest of St Andrew's Cathedral at Kronstadt. Rumours about the unusual preacher, Father John, who worked miracles with his prayers spread throughout the country. He was well-loved by believers all over Russia. "The character of John of Kronstadt is one of the most memorable in 19th century Russian history. Along with the prelate Philaret, Metropolitan of Moscow, he represents one of the high points in our religious development.

Both of these men rank alongside the great monk, Seraphim Sarovsky. Father John of Kronstadt was a wonderful complement to the other two characters – the people's priest, the people's monk, who passed his days amidst noise, rumours and tumultuous crowds, on the streets and in private homes, expressing himself in acts of charity, aid and miracles. John of Kronstadt was endowed with the highest Christian power, the gift of helping, healing prayer, the kind of gift that is the subject of obscure legends from Christianity's distant past and that Russia witnessed in the 19th century..." (Vasily Rozanov).

Petersburg has always been the home of many different religions. Nevertheless, non-Orthodox houses of worship did not appear in the city until the late 1800s. It was only at the beginning of the 20th century that a Buddhist

temple, a mosque and a number of synagogues were erected. The mosque was built on the Petrograd Side between 1910 and 1914 to designs by Nikolai Vasiliev (co-designers: Stepan Krichinsky and Alexander von Gogen). Construction was funded by donations made by Muslims throughout Russia, and considerable support came from the emir of Bukhara. The design of the northernmost mosque in the world is based upon that of various Middle Eastern buildings, particularly the mausoleum of Tamerlane in Samarkand. Inside, the building is decorated in the traditional Islamic style. Extensive use of traditional materials has been made in the exterior of the building: the dome and slender minarets are decorated with tiles, while the huge portal is covered with majolica. The bright colours of the décor lend the entire building an air of festivity and rejoicing. On overcast autumn days and in winter too, this elegant building, clearly visible even from the opposite bank of the Neva, enlivens the otherwise forbidding cityscape.

259 Dome of the mosque

260 Minaret

261 Mosque. 1910–1914, architects: Nikolai Vasiliev, Alexander von Gogen, Stepan Krichinsky

262 The cruiser *Aurora* at permanent anchor

During the 1730s, the St Petersburg Architectural Committee drew up plans not only for the main areas of the city, but also for certain new districts, including one known as Kolomna. The latter was inhabited by tradesmen, artisans, workmen and petty bureaucrats as well as employees of the Naval Office. Several interpretations of the title "Kolomna" exist of which the most popular is that it is derived from the word "colony". It is also possible that the emerging western district of the city was christened after the people of Kolomna or the inhabitants of the village of Kolomenskoye outside Moscow who were migrating to Petersburg at the time.

One of the main features of the district and the centrepiece of Labour Square (Plostchad Truda, formerly Annunciation Square) is the Nikolaevsky Palace. Intended for Nicholas I's third son, Grand Duke Nikolai Nikolaevich, inspector general of the cavalry, it was erected in conjunction with plans to bring order to the city centre as well as with the construction of the Annunciation Bridge (renamed the Nicholas Bridge in 1855 and the Lieutenant Schmidt Bridge in 1918). The palace was designed by Andrei Stackenschneider and took eight years to build from 1853 to 1861. Aware of the central role that the building was to play in the ensemble of the square, the architect endowed it with imposing dimensions and a rich decor. Inside the palace, the main staircase of the enormous vestibule with its columns of grey granite is particularly striking. The suite of lavishly decorated staterooms is also a sight to behold.

After the death of its owner in 1891, the building was sold to the state. Three years later, in honour of the marriage of Alexander III's daughter, Grand Princess Ksenia, an imperial decree was issued announcing the foundation of the Kseniinsky Institute for girls of noble birth on the premises of the Nikolaevsky Palace. This establishment was considered somewhat less prestigious than the Smolny Institute where girls from aristocratic families were educated.

THE KOLOMNA
DISTRICT

263 Fontanka River Embankment
View of the Staro-Kalinkin Bridge

→

264 Kolomna District. Mist

265 Mist on the Kriukov Canal

Petersburg is the somewhat surprising home of countless lions. Made of iron, stone and bronze, these majestic creatures are to be seen on buildings and embankments all over the city. The king of the beasts has always been favoured by ruling monarchs as a symbol of power and supremacy. In the Petrine era, the lion often played the symbolic role of the vanquished: when the Northern War put an end to Swedish rule on the banks of the Neva, the lion – an emblem of Sweden – was subject to an inevitable artistic fate. In the Summer Garden, in front of the northern façade of the Summer Palace, stands the sculptural group "Peace and Abundance" (sculptor: Pietro Baratta), an allegorical celebration of the Northern War. Russia, the victor, tramples a dying lion underfoot. Nonetheless, the mighty beast was soon reinvested with its regal qualities and took up permanent residence all over Petersburg and its environs.

266 Griboedov Canal. Lion Bridge
1825–1826, engineer: Walter Traitteur,
sculptor: Pavel Sokolov

Pupils of the Kseniinsky Institute studied such practical subjects as bookkeeping and accounting, and even specialised in the field of rail transport in accordance with a project by Andrei Stackenschneider. The last pupils graduated in 1918. The building is now the headquarters of the Trade Union Counci, and is known as the Palace of Labour.

The early 18th century architect Piotr Eropkin, the mastermind behind the layout of the city centre, also designed the large timber warehouses on the islet known as New Holland. In the 1760s – 1780s the "geometry" of the natural channels and artificial canals was perfected by Vallin de La Mothe, who gave the entire complex a truly august appearance. The unusual beauty of New Holland captured the attention of artists and writers alike. The famous local scholar and area studies specialist, Nikolai Antsiferov, wrote of this unique work of art: "On the Moika is an island enclosed by a high red wall. It is divided in two by the canal, above which towers a splendid arch worthy of the Eternal City. It soars elegantly over the canal as if beckoning victorious galleys to pass beneath it. It stands here in a remote part of town, evidently out of place. The masts of ships show up black beneath it against the perpetual twilight of the White Nights. And it seems like a kind of apparition."

→
270–276 Wrought iron designs
on the embankments and bridges
of Petersburg

→ →
277. Panoramic view
of the Moika River

278 Moika River Embankment

The most famous residence on the Moika is the Yusupov Palace. Here, on the night of 16 December 1916, Grigory Rasputin was murdered in a prologue to the bloody events of 1917. In the eyes of Nicholas II and his wife Alexandra Fedorovna, the Siberian peasant, seer and miracle worker embodied a mystic link between the Orthodox tsar and the people. Having lost the support of the upper echelons of society, the Russian autocrat hoped to curry favour with the common people with the aid of the monk. Rasputin himself was aware that he was the royal family's last hope not only to stay on the throne, but also, with his apparent psychic powers, to preserve the health of the heir

279 Yusupov Palace. 1830–1838, architect: Andrei Mikhailov

280 Yusupov Palace. Moorish Drawing Room

281 Yusupov Palace. Theatre

apparent, who suffered from haemophilia. Some were convinced that Rasputin was a clairvoyant and a prophet, the guardian angel of the royal family and of Russia as a whole. To others he was a play-acting adventurer, a perverted debauchee, a political intriguer and swindler who used religion to cover his deeds. Vexed by Rasputin's influence over the tsar, aristocrats and representatives of the royal circles alike felt compelled to take extreme measures. A conspiracy arose, and members of distinguished families, including Grand Duke Dmitry Pavlovich, Prince Felix Yusupov the

282 Felix and Irina Yusupov. Photograph

283 Valentin Serov. 1865–1911. *Portrait of Zinaida Yusupova.* 1902

284 Grigory Rasputin. Photograph

285 Yusupov Palace. The Princess's Boudoir

Younger and Vladimir Purishkevich, a monarchist and an outspoken member of the State Duma (parliament), finally sought to assassinate the "holy man". In the palace basement is the room to which Felix Yusupov lured Rasputin in order to implement their brutal plan. Legend has it that neither poisoned cakes, nor two shots from a revolver, nor a fierce blow to the head were sufficient to kill him. It was not until Rasputin was thrown into the river that he finally died. This man and his murder are the subject of one of the last myths of Imperial Petersburg.

The first in the ancient line of the Yusupovs to own the palace, rebuilt in the 1830s from an 18th century domicile by the architect Andrei Mikhailov, was Prince Nikolai Borisovich, a dignitary during the reign of Catherine the Great. This fabulously wealthy art lover had a serf theatre that was famous in its day, and also owned a splendid collection of paintings and other works of art. He survived four reigning monarchs and was a knight of all the orders of Russia. Under Nicholas I, he was awarded with the pearl epaulette, a unique decoration devised especially for him. His wife, Tatiana Vasilievna, a relative of Grigory Potemkin, collected precious stones. Her treasures included the famous diamond known as the "Pole Star", Philip II of Spain's "Peregrine" (a pearl), and Marie-Antoinette's earrings.

The palace's last owner was Count Felix Sumarokov-Elston the Elder, otherwise known as Prince Yusupov. He has awarded the title of prince with the approval of Alexander III when he married the last surviving member of the Yusupov family, Zinaida Nikolaevna. She was very wealthy and unusually attractive. Indeed, her contemporaries deemed her beauty "the symbol of an era". Their youngest son, Felix, went down in history as an active participant in Rasputin's murder.

The interiors of the residence, particularly the White Hall, the Ballroom, the Large Rotunda, the Red and Blue Drawing Rooms, the Turkish Study, the Moorish Drawing Room and the main staircase are stunningly beautiful and lavishly decorated. The unique Household Theatre, a miniature replica of an 18th–19th century playhouse, is also worthy of note.

After the revolution, an art gallery was opened in the palace, but the entire collection of paintings was soon transferred to the Hermitage and the building handed over to the Union of Educational Workers. Following the war and subsequent restoration work, the residence, which had been badly damaged by bombs and shells, became the Regional House of Teachers.

286 Fontanka River Embankment. Mist

The Mariinsky Theatre opened its first season on 2 October 1860 with Glinka's opera "A Life for the Tsar". Music by the famous Russian composers Nikolai Rimsky-Korsakov, Modest Mussorgsky and Piotr Tchaikovsky would be heard for the first time within its walls. For over fifty years, its magnificent orchestra was led by the composer and conductor Eduard Napravnik. The theatre's huge stage made it possible to put on performances involving large casts and intricate scenery. The last third of the 19th century was the most successful period in the Mariinsky Theatre's pre-Revolutionary existence, during which it hosted productions by Marius Petipa. The dancers Mathilda Kshesinskaya, Anna Pavlova, Tamara Karsavina, Vatslav Nijinsky and Mikhail Fokin brought these spectacles great acclaim. The Russian school of opera also developed in the Mariinsky. Leading roles were performed by Leonid Sobinov and Fedor Chaliapin, who made his debut on 5 April 1895 in Charles Gounod's opera "Faust". During this period, the scenery for many of the productions was created by the artists Alexander Benois, Konstantin Korovin and Alexander Golovin, who, in 1914, designed the stage curtain that hangs in the theatre to this day.

287 Mariinsky Theatre
1847–1849, 1859, architect: Albert Kavos;
1883–1886, 1894, architect: Viktor Shroeter

288, 289 Mariinsky Theatre
Auditorium

In the early 20th century, many of the Mariinksy's soloists starred in Serguei Diaghilev's "Russian Seasons". It is through his efforts that Western Europe became acquainted with Russian musical and artistic culture, which exercised a considerable influence on the development of world ballet.

After the October Revolution, a new era began in the history of the Mariinsky Theatre. A different team of performers, musicians and conductors emerged, and productions on contemporary themes began to rule the stage.

It is here that Galina Ulanova embarked upon her artistic career. For a long time, the leading solo dancers were Natalia Dudinskaya and Konstantin Sergueev. The famous Agrippina Vaganova also performed on the stage of the Mariinsky.

With the coming of the famous musician Valery Gerguiev, many interesting experimental productions began to be staged, testifying to a relentless search for innovative forms in the fields of opera and ballet as well as the art of set design.

290 *Sleeping Beauty*
at the Mariinsky Theatre

291 *Boris Godunov*
at the Mariinsky Theatre

292, 293 Uliana Lopatkina, Igor Zelensky, Farukh Rusimatov: leading lights of the Mariinsky Theatre

The famous Mariinsky Theatre, named in honour of Alexander II's wife, became Petersburg's principal theatre of opera and ballet in the second half of the 19th century. The theatre was first designed by Albert Kavos. In the 1880s–1890s, however, it was remodelled under the direction of Viktor Shroeter and given the external appearance it has today.

The traditions of the famous stage and the rich history of expertise are painstakingly upheld within the theatre's walls. Its ballet troupe and many of its opera singers are not only well known in Russia, but also admired all over the world. The Mariinsky Theatre was and still is an integral part of the cultural life of Petersburg and Russia.

The area of town in which the St Nicholas Cathedral, or "Sailor's Church", stands today was once occupied by quarters for members of the Naval Department. A square that initially served as the parade ground for the Admiralty was to become the centre of this part of Petersburg and a church was erected upon it. The building project was funded by tolls taken at the St Isaac's Bridge over the Neva. The first service was held in the St Nicholas Cathedral on 14 September 1770, following the defeat of the Turkish armada at Chesma Bay. Built from 1753 to 1762 to designs by Savva Chevakinsky, a contemporary of the great 18th-century

294 Kriukov Canal
View of the St Nicholas Cathedral complex

295 St Nicholas Cathedral
1753–1762, architect: Savva Chevakinsky

Petersburg architect Bartolomeo Rastrelli, this church is one of the city's most outstanding architectural monuments. It is remarkable for its well-preserved interior into which Chevakinsky incorporated traits of palace architecture. Following the Russian tradition, there are two churches in the cathedral. The upper, Theophany Church is used mainly on Sundays and on the days of religious feasts and

296 St Nicholas Cathedral
Interior of the Upper Church

297 St Nicholas Cathedral
Icon: *St Nicholas the Miracle Worker*

has a brighter, airy feel and a typically Baroque exuberance. The lower (winter) church, intended for daily use, is lit by icon lamps, candles and chandeliers, creating a magical effect. Thus, the pale blue and gold two-storey edifice with its five domes is a splendid sight both inside and out. The interior of the church is richly decorated with gilt carving, particularly fine examples of which are to be seen on the iconostasis dating from 1755–1760. Sculptures and columns wreathed with carved garlands also feature heavily in the design of the icon screen. An icon of St Nicholas, one of the most popular saints in Russia, where he is known as "Nicholas the Miracle Worker", is to be found inside the St Nicholas Cathedral. Nicholas is regarded as the saint who is "swift to aid". He is always depicted on icons as a balding old man dressed in robes that indicate his venerable status as a clergyman. His figure is typically shown full-length with his right hand raised in blessing and his left holding the Gospels.

An important part of the architectural ensemble of the St Nicholas Cathedral is the freestanding four-tiered belfry, which with its beautiful lines ranks amongst the most sublime works of Russian architecture. Elegant and well-proportioned, crowned with a small, graceful dome and spire, it strikes the viewer as somehow at one with the smooth waters of the nearby Kriukov Canal in which it is reflected on clear days and bright summer nights.

298 St Nicholas Cathedral at night

299 Red Guards Bridge in the vicinity of the St Nicholas Cathedral

→

300 Griboedov Canal. Granite pier. Flood

301 Griboedov Canal (formerly the Catherine Canal)

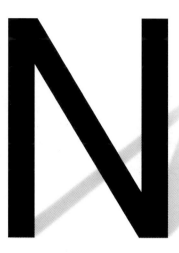evsky Prospekt ends at Vosstaniya (Insurrection) Square, giving way to Old Nevsky Prospekt, which leads to the St Alexander Nevsky Monastery.

Founded by order of Peter I in 1710, the St Alexander Nevsky Monastery is almost as old as the city itself. It was named in honour of St Alexander Nevsky, an outstanding 13th century holy prince and statesman who was declared patron saint of St Petersburg by the Orthodox Church. Under his command, the Russian army triumphed over the Swedes on the banks of the Neva in 1240.

Peter I decided to transfer the relics of the Orthodox Russian warrior who ranked amongst the heavenly hosts to the new capital. Thus, work began on the urgent construction of the Alexander Nevsky Holy Trinity Monastery far beyond the confines of the city. In 1797, it was declared a "lavra", the term used to describe the most important Orthodox monasteries.

The monastery was linked to the city by a single road that led up to a small river known as the Ligovka. When laying the road, the monks miscalculated somewhat and set it at an angle to the long straight line of Nevsky Prospekt, which led down to the river from the north. In the 19th century, the Ligovka was filled in. Today, in its place runs Ligovsky Prospekt.

The oldest building within the monastery is the two-storey Church of the Annunciation. It was built from 1717 to 1722, and it was to this place that the relics of the military leader were brought on 30 August 1724 to be laid in the Alexander Nevsky Church on the first floor. Later, a splendid silver shrine was built for them, which can now be seen in the Hermitage.

Within the walls of the St Alexander Nevsky Monastery, on either side of the main entrance, lies a pair of cemeteries. To the left is the 18th-century St Lazarus Cemetery, the oldest graveyard in the city, which first came into being in the Petrine era, when permission for internment

ST ALEXANDER
NEVSKY MONASTERY
AND CHURCHES
OF PETERSBURG

302 Panoramic view
of the St Alexander Nevsky Monastery

After the opening of the Tikhvin Cemetery, the remains of many famous 18th century Russian artists and writes were transferred to this spot.

On 1 February 1881, Fedor Dostoevsky was laid to rest here. The suggestion to bury the Russian writer in the Tikhvin Cemetery was made by a representative of the monastery, who said that the monks "ask that a place be granted for free, and would consider it an honour if the ashes of the writer Dostoevsky, who zealously defended the Orthodox faith, were to lie within the walls of the lavra." A headstone was placed over the writer's grave in 1883. This monument was designed by the architect Chrisanf Vasiliev and shows a bust of Dostoevsky (sculptor: Nikolai Laveretsky) against the background of a granite pillar surmounted with a cross. In the northern part of the Tikhvin Cemetery, the outstanding Russian composer Piotr Tchaikovsky was buried in 1893. The monument that marks his grave (sculptor: Pavel Kamensky), enclosed by an intricate grille, was erected 4 years later.

On a slab of granite shaped like a piece of cliff stands a bronze bust of the composer shielded by the wings of an angel bearing a cross.

In the 1930s, it was decided to turn the Tikhvin Cemetery into a Necropolis of Famous Men of Culture. The area underwent serious renovation and monuments that were of no artistic value were removed. After a network of avenues and paths had been laid, the cemetery began to resemble a park.

303 St Alexand
Entrance

304 Dostoevsky's grave
1883, sculptor: Nikolai Laveretsky

305 Tchaikovsky's tomb
1897, sculptor: Piotr Kamensky

had to be obtained from the tsar. This cemetery was set aside for the burial of members of the nobility, high-ranking officials and wealthy merchants only. The places of honour were considered to be along the walls of the burial-vault of the Lazarev. It was here that a number of Russian artists were laid to rest, including the architects Ivan Starov, Andrean Zakharov, Andrei Voronikhin, Giacomo Quarenghi and Carlo Rossi, the sculptors Fedot Shubin and Feodosy Shchedrin, and the artists Vladimir Borovikovsky and Silvester Shchedrin. The fascinating sculptural monuments that adorn the graves were created by such prominent Russian masters of the plastic arts as Ivan Martos, Mikhail Kozlovsky, Fedot Shubin and others.

In 1832, the Tikhvin Cemetery was opened to the right of the entrance to the monastery. Many Russian writers, artists, composers and performers are buried here. Throughout the 18th century, a number of famous architects worked on the Alexander Nevsky Holy

Trinity Monastery, transforming it into an architectural ensemble that comprised buildings of different eras and styles. The construction of the monastery was completed by the renowned Russian architect Ivan Starov.

Starov designed the main entrance to the St Alexander Nevsky Monastery, which opens out onto a square that is also his work. The architect demarcated its boundaries on one side with a pair of residential buildings that stand at the end of Old Nevsky Prospekt, while on the other side he placed a stone wall. In the centre of the semicircular square, the architect built a church over the gate — Church of the Icon of the Mother of God "The Joy of All Who Sorrow" (1783–1785) with an arch and symmetrical apses in the eastern (the altar end) and western sections. The western apse contains a staircase leading to the upper church.

Starov also created the central building of the St Alexander Nevsky Monastery, the majestic Trinity Cathedral,

306 St Alexander Nevsky Monastery. St Theodore Church. 1740–1750, architect: Pietro Trezzini

307 St Alexander Nevsky Monastery. Church of the Annunciation. 1717–1722, architect: Domenico Trezzini

308 St Alexander Nevsky Monastery. Inner courtyard

which plays an important symbolic and compositional role in the monastery ensemble. The new cathedral was built to Starov's designs from 1776–1790 in place of an existing church whose walls had begun to crack. The Trinity Cathedral, which boasts two monumental belfries, is an example of religious architecture in the style of late 18th-century Russian Classicism. Sculptural panels created by Fedot Shubin can be seen above the side entrances. Shubin too was responsible for the statues of the saints that stand inside the church. The gilded bronze gates of the iconostasis of the Trinity Cathedral are of remarkable elegance and beauty.

Architectural accents are highly characteristic of the overall design of Petersburg. To begin with this role was played by the two towering spires of the Admiralty and the Peter and Paul Fortress. Later, the cupolas of religious buildings came to perform a similar function.

309 St Alexander Nevsky Monastery
Holy Trinity Cathedral
Central nave

310 St Alexander Nevsky Monastery
Holy Trinity Cathedral. 1776–1790,
architect: Ivan Starov

265

As dominant features of the skyline in various areas of Petersburg, they played a fundamental part in shaping the appearance of the city and in many ways determined the plastic expressiveness of their environment and brought variety to the cityscape. In Petersburg, the long horizontal lines of the rivers, canals and streets, lined with buildings of almost uniform height, are broken by the verticals of belfries, spires and cupolas of various shapes and sizes.

The architecture of the churches of Petersburg is magnificent. The enormous dome of St Isaac's, visible from as far away as Kronstadt in the Finnish Gulf, prevails over half of the city. The St Nicholas Cathedral and its graceful four-tiered belfry looks elegant and festive from all angles and at all times of the year, while the Church on the Spilled Blood blooms at the end of Griboedov Canal like a rare and exotic perennial flower, stunning the viewer with its riot of colours and intricate architectural forms.

Monuments to active religious sentiment are also to be found in Petersburg. Amongst the most prominent of these is the chapel that stands over the grave of Xenia the Blessed (1900, architect: Alexander Vseslavin), the Russian saint and "fool for Christ" who acquired a cult following amongst the common people of Petersburg in the 18th century. Even in the most godless years of Soviet Russia,

311 Chapel of St Xenia the Blessed
1900, architect: Alexander Vseslavin

312 Church of the Smolensk Icon
of the Mother of God. 1786–1790,
architect: A. Ivanov

313 Chapel of St Xenia the Blessed
Icon: *St Xenia the Blessed of Petersburg*

314 Dome of the Church of the
Smolensk Icon of the Mother of God

hundreds of people would come to pray at her grave, asking her to intercede for them before the Lord or lend assistance in earthly matters. The chapel is situated in the grounds of the Smolensk Cemetery on Vasilievsky Island. To this day, the church within the cemetery contains a holy relic of Russian Orthodoxy, the miracle-working Smolensk icon of the Mother of God, to which the church owes its name.

Having ascended the throne, Peter I abolished the patriarchate and installed an "ecclesiastical board" known as the Holy Synod at the head of the church. This institution was overseen by the chief procurator, a lay official appointed by the Emperor himself.

During the Petersburg era of Russian history, the Orthodox Church practically became a state organ. One of the signs of the Church's subordination to the state was the consecration of churches in the name of "calendar saints" who shared the names of Emperors,

or in honour of saints, whose days coincided with the dates of events that were significant to the state, such as a military victory, for example. The Church of Sts Simeon and Anna (1731–1734, architect: Mikhail Zemtsov) was built during the reign of Anna Ioannovna. The defeat of the Turks at Chesma Bay in 1770 was marked by the founding of the Church of the Nativity of St John the Baptist (1777–1780, architect: Yury Velten), better known as the Chesma Church. St Petersburg is also the home of a cathedral consecrated in the name of Prince Vladimir, who was canonised in the days of Ancient Rus (1741–1772, architects: Mikhail Zemtsov, Pietro Trezzini, Antonio Rinaldi).

At the beginning of 1917 there were over 700 churches and chapels in Petersburg. Now there are approximately 100. A number of these religious buildings, such as the Church of the Resurrection on the bank of Obvodny Canal (1904–1908, architects: Grimm,

315 St Trinity Cathedral. 1828–1835, architect: Vasily Stasov

von Goli, and Gun) have now been handed back to the Church and, thanks to the efforts of restorers, their interiors have been recreated. Many of the churches and cathedrals were preserved simply because they were declared sites of artistic value.

316 Kazan Icon of the Mother of God (the holy icon was transferred from Holy Prince Vladimir's Cathedral to the Kazan Cathedral in July 2001)

317 Holy Prince Vladimir's Cathedral. 1741–1772, architect: Mikhail Zemtsov, Pietro Trezzini, Antonio Rinaldi

318 St Samson's Cathedral. 1728–1740

The best period of Petersburg church architecture, namely the 18th and early 19th century, is characterised by untraditional and "non-Orthodox" traits. Many of the religious buildings dating from this time resemble the Catholic edifices of Rome, while the fantastical "Gothic" structure of the Chesma Church is totally unique.

Churches in Petersburg often bear the names of secular departments. The Cathedral of the Transfiguration, for example, was built in 1743–1754 as the regimental church of the Preobrazhensky ("Transfiguration") Guards who took part in the palace coup that resulted in Elizabeth Petrovna's ascension to the throne. The original church burned down in 1825. Its replacement, designed by Vasily Stasov, has survived to this day. The completion of the Transfiguration Cathedral coincided with a victory in the Russo-Turkish War, thus Stasov used the Turkish cannons that had been seized in battle to create a unique fence around the church.

The former Trinity Cathedral within the settlement of the Izmailovsky Regiment was also remodelled in accordance with plans by Vasily Stasov. In the New Izmailovsky Cathedral built in 1835, the architect retained the original arrangement of the cupolas, which mark the four points of the compass. A Monument to Glory consisting of the barrels of trophy weapons stacked in the form of a pyramid once stood in front of the church.

319 Chesma Church of the Nativity of St John the Baptist. 1777–1780, architect: Yury Velten

320 Chesma Church
Detail of the façade

Each church in Petersburg that did not cease to serve a religious function after the Revolution has its own object of worship. In the Cathedral of the Transfiguration this is the icon – "the Image Not-Made-By-Hands of Our Lord Jesus Christ". The latter is a highly important image of the Saviour that was created, as legend has it, during the life of Christ and at His will. As the story goes, the artist Ananias was sent by his seriously ill king to draw Christ's portrait, but was unable to fulfil his task because the light emanating from the God-Man made it too difficult to pick out His features. Instead, Christ requested a clean cloth and, having washed His face, wiped it on the fabric. An outline of the Saviour's visage remained miraculously imprinted upon the cloth. It is said that the icon has the power to aid and protect the faithful since it was created in the act of saving a suffering man. In Ancient Rus, the "Image Not-Made-By-Hands of Our Lord Jesus Christ" was often hung over the gates of fortresses or depicted on military standards. The holy relic of the Cathedral of the Transfiguration originally belonged to Peter I and was his favourite and most revered icon. The Emperor carried it with him whenever he was travelling or engaged in military campaigns. The religious image hung in Peter the Great's House until Elizabeth Petrovna bestowed it upon the Cathedral of the Transfiguration.

321 Cathedral of the Transfiguration 1743–1754, architects: Mikhail Zemtsov, Pietro Trezzini: 1828–1829, architect: Vasily Stasov

322 Vladimir Church. 1761–1769 Belfry. 1783, architect: Giacomo Quarenghi

323 Cathedral of the Transfiguration Icon of the Image Not-Made-By-Hands of Our Lord Jesus Christ

The palaces and residences built in the Baroque style by the court architect Bartolomeo Francesco Rastrelli adorn the city to this day. One such work is the ensemble of the Smolny Convent (1748–1764) situated on the upper left-hand bank of the Neva at a bend in the river.

Although Rastrelli was unable to bring his original plan entirely to fruition, it is possible to imagine the beauty and originality of his proposed ensemble from the magnificent buildings that can be seen today. The expressiveness of the composition and the perfection of both the individual components and the whole make it one of the high points in world architecture. The centrepiece of the convent, both literally and structurally, was the cathedral.

"At the time of Swedish rule, the place where the cathedral stands was occupied by the settlement of Spasskoye, where Orthodox men of letters lived and a chapel stood. After Peter had conquered this territory, a large tar yard was built. Later, a country palace was erected here for Elizabeth and christened "Smolny" (meaning *tar*). Legend has it that in the fourth year of her reign, Elizabeth intended to hand the reins of government to her nephew, Peter III, and end her days peacefully in a convent. Cherishing this thought, she ordered the construction of a religious retreat for women on the spot where her palace stood, to be named the Convent of the Resurrection. The plans and construction work were entrusted to Rastrelli. The foundations of the convent were laid on 30 October 1748 after a fire had destroyed the main wing of the Empress's palace" (Mikhail Pyliaev).

The architect envisaged the convent as a "regular" part of "regular" Petersburg. All of the convent buildings are laid out symmetrically. In the centre stands the lofty cathedral, while around the edge of the courtyard run the living quarters with small "domestic" churches at each corner.

The Smolny Convent is enclosed by a wall. Even in the very early days of Rus, convents were surrounded by thick walls that offered protection from both worldly temptations and

324 Panoramic view
of the Smolny Monastery

hostile attackers. In Rastrelli's 18th century ensemble, how-ever, the walls were a tribute to tradition rather than a defence mechanism.

By order of the Empress, the cathedral of the Smolny Convent was erected after the Orthodox tradition and en-dowed with five cupolas. It is divided into two parts, of which the lower looks like an idiosyncratic and mighty pedestal for the five cupolas, each in turn standing on its own base. The small cupolas are set very close to the central dome, which lends the entire edifice a certain compositional integrity. When designing the facades, the architect paid careful attention to a very important spatial issue: the cathedral was supposed to appear picturesque from any point in the convent courtyard. Thus, Rastrelli gave each façade a special appearance. The face of the building is unusual for the combination of different geo-metric forms worked into and protruding from it.

By 1764, only the framework of the cathedral was com-plete, but even that was sufficient to inspire rapture in all who saw it. The famous Giacomo Quarenghi, who was largely scep-tical about the Baroque style, doffed his hat while walking past the Smolny Convent one day and said: "Now there's a church!"

"Eighty years after the laying of the foundations, the mag-nificent building of the cathedral stood unfinished, and it was not consecrated until 20 June 1835 at the wish of the most august mother of Emperor Nicholas I" (Mikhail Pyliaev). In the 1830s, the task of completing the construction and decorating the interior of the cathedral was given to Vasily Stasov. His austere white interior contrasts dramatically with the lavish exterior.

The Cathedral of the Resurrection in the Smolny Con-vent looks particularly striking both from the water and from the opposite bank. It rises up like a magical vision, sparkling with gilt and stunning the viewer with the bright blue of its walls, the intricacy of its cupolas and the beauty and elegance of its entire countenance.

Further along the left bank of the Neva stands a palace that was built for Catherine II's favourite, Grigory Potemkin

325 Smolny Cathedral. 1748–1769, architect: Bartolomeo Rastrelli

326 View of the Smolny Cathedral in winter

(1783–1789, architect: Ivan Starov). Potemkin was commander-in-chief of the Russian army during the Russo-Turkish War, which culminated in the conquest of the mouth of the Black Sea, for which the military leader was awarded the title of Prince of Tauride (the early name for the Crimea). After Potemkin's death, the Empress wrote that: "He was a person of great mind, rare intellect and a superior heart; his aims were always centred upon the great."

When Potemkin died in 1791, Catherine reclaimed the palace for the state in order to turn it into a residence for the royal family. On 7 September 1792, it was christened the Tauride Palace in honour of its former owner. Catherine was particularly fond of spending the spring months here. When Paul I came to the throne he converted his mother's residence into stables and barracks for the Horseguards. Nonetheless, during the reign of Catherine's favourite grandson, Alexander I, the palace regained its former splendour. In 1917, it became the home of both the Provisional Government and the

327 Tauride Palace. 1783–1789, architect: Ivan Starov

328 Mikhail Ivanov. 1728–1823
*Prince Potemkin with a Cavalry Detachment
on the Neva Embankment*. 1798

329 Tauride Palace. Columned Hall

Petrograd Soviet of Workers' and Soldiers' Deputies. Today, the Parliamentary Commission of the CIS countries meets here.

The design of the Tauride Palace consists of three basic components, a central corpus linked by galleries to a pair of side pavilions. This type of building served as a model for many estates in Russia.

The left bank of the Neva is also graced by a building that dates from the first third of the 18th century. At one time it belonged to the naval adviser Alexander Kikin, who was one of Peter the Great's associates. When Peter learned of Kikin's involvement in the affairs of the tsarevich Alexis, the Emperor dealt with the admiral severely: he was arrested and subsequently put to death. Kikin's home was confiscated, and a collection of Peter I's rarities was installed there. Hence, the Kikin Mansion may be deemed the first museum in Petersburg, the predecessor to the Kunstkammer. In the 1950s, following a restoration project led by the architect Irina Benois, the building came to resemble its former self once more.

Prince Alexander Bezborodko, a famous dignitary during the reign of Catherine the Great, was, according to his contemporaries, "an agile mind in a cumbersome body." For his

330 Kikin Mansion. 1714–1720

331 Bezborodko Villa. 1773–1777, architect: Vasily Bazhenov; 1783–1784, architect: Giacomo Quarenghi

332 Sverdlovsk Embankment. Stone lions outside the Bezborodko Villa

diplomatic services, Catherine II made him one of her secret advisors and awarded him the order of St Andrew. Paul I later promoted him to the position of chancellor of state. Bezborodko was a wealthy man who had a home in Petersburg as well as a villa in Polyustrovo (now within the bounds of the city). This country residence was designed by Vasily Bazhenov and remodelled slightly in 1783–1784 by Giacomo Quarenghi.

The Prince was renowned for his "rakish lifestyle and frivolous affairs with women, whom he always admired passionately and indiscriminately." At his villa, he kept a serf theatre that was more like a harem. His liaisons with the actresses were often scandalous. Bezborodko also spent vast amounts of money on the Italian ballerina, Anna Bernucci, "giving her a monthly allowance of 8,000 roubles in gold." This aroused the displeasure of Catherine II, who ordered that the dancer be expelled from Russia within 24 hours.

*As it wends its smooth and leisurely way, the Neva assumes a number of very different guises. From the Lieutenant Schimdt and Tuchkov Bridges right up to the Smolny Convent it is a stately, cosmopolitan river. Here, all of the architectural beauty of old Petersburg is to be seen lining its banks. Up to these bridges and beyond the Smolny stretches the working river, marked by the cranes of the freight port, the masts of boats in the shipyards and the industrial chimneys at the mouth of the Neva. At night, the Neva does not belong to the city of Petersburg alone: it once again becomes a part of the ancient waterway that stretched "from the Varangians to the Greeks", linking four seas with inland Russia. During the small hours, when the bridges are raised, large ships enter the bounds of the city. They proceed past the monument to the first Russian seafarer to sail around the world in 1802, Admiral Ivan Krusenstern. The statue stands opposite the home of the Naval Cadet Corps, which was once under Krusenstern's direction.
Saint Petersburg has stood out from other Russian cities from time immemorial. It owes its uniqueness first and foremost to its geographical location: Petersburg stands on the edge of the vast territory of Russia and is indeed a "window onto Europe". From the west it has not only been buffeted by the turbulent waters of the autumn floods, but also by the shockwaves of historic disasters endured on the continent, while traces of European ideas and the joys and woes of the "old continent" have been borne in on the Baltic winds.*

333 Bolsheokhtinsky Bridge
(Peter the Great Bridge). 1908–1911

→

334 Panorama of the Neva

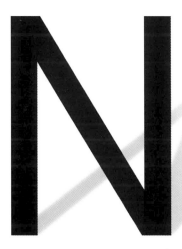N o description of St Petersburg would be complete without some mention of the former imperial residences that are strung out around the edges of the northern capital like the beads of an exquisite necklace.

Many of these park and palace complexes came into being at the same time as the city and, in accordance with Peter I's plans, became a delightful and fitting frame for Petersburg. Each of the country residences has its own unique and special charm and each one reflects the aesthetic tastes of different historical eras, which have been added to and altered with time. Although all of the country residences have retained evidence of the personal predilections of their various owners, the majority of them are largely associated with one or other ruler in particular.

The most deserving of our attention is Peterhof, the favourite residence of Peter I, after whom it is named. Peterhof constitutes a grandiose 18th–19th century architectural and park ensemble with an area of over a thousand hectares dotted with approximately thirty buildings and pavilions and decorated with over one hundred sculptures.

The Emperor was a regular visitor to the naval fortress at Kronstadt. However, the path to the latter, which lay over the sea, was dangerous and uncomfortable. Thus, Catherine I, who always accompanied her husband on his travels, as legend has it, asked Peter to build a convenient stopping point on the shore of the gulf. The idea captured the tsar's active imagination and he decided to create a lavish residence. He personally chose the spot on which it was to be built and drew up plans for the layout of the park, buildings and fountains. Peter envisaged Peterhof not only as a place to rest and receive guests. The Emperor conceived it as a monument to the transfiguration of Russia, to its glorious victory in the Northern War with Sweden.

15 August 1723 saw the official opening of Peterhof. Its three palaces (the Upper Chambers, the Marly and Monplaisir), two cascades and 16 fountains set in a regular

PETERHOF

335 View of the Grand Canal (otherwise known as the Sea or Samson Canal)

park left visitors stunned by their splendour. The arrangement of fountains on the terraces and in the lower park was developed in the Petrine era. At the time, these unique ornaments were given different shapes and sizes in order to achieve an array of effects with the falling water. By skilfully exploiting the lay of the extensive territory with its natural ledges, slopes and plains, architects, engineers and sculptors succeeded in creating a picturesque park and peerless architectural ensemble.

The Grand Cascade was first brought into action in 1723, but at the end of the 18th – beginning of the 19th century, a great deal of work had to be done to replace the damaged lead sculptures. It was at this time that seventeen bronze copies of antique originals were incorporated into the composition of the cascade. These include the "Wounded Amazon", "Ganymede", "Cupid and Psyche" and "Medici Venus". The latter is a recognised artistic representation of the goddess of love, which shows her emerging from the sea, her half-naked body frozen in a twisted pose. Of particular value are the fifteen original bronze statues that were designed by Russian masters and pupils of the Academy of Arts, which include, for example, Fedot Shubin's "Perseus". In the Petrine era this mythical hero who vanquished over a sea-monster was used as an allegory for the Russian tsar who defeated the Swedish army. Meanwhile, the rescued Andromeda was likened to the lands that were returned to Russia.

The centrepiece of the Great Cascade is the fountain of "Samson Tearing Open the Jaws of the Lion", which was created in honour of the 25th anniversary of an important

336 View of the Grand Cascade

337 Panorama of the Great Palace and Grand Cascade

Russian victory. On 27 June 1709, St Samson's Day, the famous Poltava Battle took place in which the Russian army, led by Peter I, routed King Charles XII of Sweden's troops. The aforesaid sculpture was to serve as an allegorical expression of Russia's triumph over Sweden, a task that naturally dictated the monument's design. The pious saint was transformed in the Russian interpretation into a mighty Biblical character, and the king of the beasts, which appears on the Swedish coat of arms, inevitably came to represent the northern aggressor. A twenty-metre high jet of water shoots from the jaws of the lion like a victorious salvo. The sculpture was originally created by Carlo Rastrelli, but was replaced in 1801 by the work of Mikhail Kozlovsky.

The architect Bartolomeo Rastrelli played a fundamental role in transforming the Upper Chambers, built back in the Petrine era, into the impressive formal edifice known today as the Great Palace. The latter swiftly became the compositional and artistic centrepiece of the Upper and Lower Parks. The interiors too were refurbished according to Rastrelli's designs, and both the use of space and the décor itself were in perfect accord with the purpose served by the palace.

338 Grand Cascade. West staircase

339 Grand Cascade
Fountain: *Samson Tearing Open the Jaws of the Lion*
1801, sculptor: Mikhail Kozlovsky; cast by V. Ekimov

In front of the northern façade of the palace, stretching down towards the sea, is the Lower Garden, which embraces a variety of buildings together with the Grand Cascade, two smaller cascades and numerous fountains. At the centre of this magnificent symmetrical composition is the Grand Cascade. It looks particularly striking from the water. Besides the fountains themselves, sculptures and basreliefs play an important symbolic and ornamental part in the Grand Cascade ensemble. In the form of allegories, they represent and celebrate Russia's military prowess and naval might. The entire composition bristles with a total of 38 statues and 213 bas-reliefs, busts, mascarons and urns. The images portrayed in the sculptures and the subjects of the basreliefs are taken from ancient mythology. At the time of Peter I's reign, Greek antiquity in its Roman interpretation provided the chief stock of themes employed in Russian art. It was the Emperor himself who laid the foundations for this preoccupation with antiquity, and the Emperor too who acquired the first antique relic to appear in Russia, namely a statue of Venus. From that moment on, collecting antiques became a popular pastime amongst the educated nobility.

340 Grand Cascade
Decorative sculpture:
Wounded Amazon. 1801, sculptor:
Fedor Gordeev. Copy from
an antique original dating from
the 5th-4th century BC

341 Grand Cascade. Decorative
sculpture: *Ganymede*. 1800
Copy from an antique original
by Leochares. Cast by Edmonde
Gastecloux

Peterhof is famed largely for its
fountains, which are both
ingenious works of hydraulic
engineering and masterpieces
of monumental decorative art.
The glittering, iridescent jets
of the three cascades and the
many fountains playing in the
rays of the sun create the unique
sensation of a celebration
of nature and the apotheosis
of Peter the Great's own
favourite element – water.
The variety of forms and
the different functions played
by the fountains make Peterhof
an open-air museum unlike
any other in the world.
Each of the ornamental fountains in the grounds is the "hero"
of a particular subject. "Adam"
and "Eve" remind visitors that
they are in a veritable earthly
paradise. "The Favourite"
is an illustration of La Fontaine's
fable about a dog trying to catch
ducks. Finally, the sculptural
ornaments of the Grand Cascade make up a complete
allegorical tale of the victories
won over the enemies of Petrine
Russia and at the same time
celebrate the nation's entry into
the European political arena.

342 Grand Cascade. Basket Fountain
(1860, architect: Nikolai Benois) and
the entrance to the Small Grotto

343 Decorative sculptures
inside the Large Grotto

The Great Palace is the main building of the Peterhof ensemble. Although its appearance was shaped over the course of almost half a century, the basic threefold structure of the building was determined from the outset. In the mid-18th century, while preserving the basic design, Rastrelli enlarged the palace and thereby lent it a majestic air. The central three-storey component, in which only the middle section of the Petrine Upper Chambers remains, is linked by ground floor galleries to the two-storey side wings. To the west is the Coat of Arms Wing, so named because of the traditional emblem of the two-headed eagle perched atop the domed roof of the building. The coat of arms is 27 metres off the ground and a special device enables it to rotate like a weather vane. The figure of the eagle is ingeniously contrived: the presence of an extra head enables it to appear in all its double-headed glory no matter which way it turns. To the east, the architectural composition terminates in the Church, which is crowned with a central dome and a number of smaller gilded cupolas.

344 View of the Great Palace and Grand Cascade from the Grand Canal

345 View of the Grand Cascade ensemble from the Voronikhin Colonnade

Inside the Great Palace, the staterooms and drawing rooms are located on the first floor. Rastrelli made the largest of these the Throne Room, which has an area of 300 metres. A double row of windows reflected in a series of mirrors visually increases the size of the hall. A large number of windows of different shapes and sizes interspersed with strategically placed mirrors were a common device used in Baroque architecture to create the illusion of endless space and eliminate the boundary between the interior and the surrounding grounds.

346 Great Palace. Ballroom

347 Great Palace. Throne Room
1763–1780

348 View of the Grand Canal from
the windows of the Great Palace

The staterooms at Peterhof are characterised by a superabundance of paintings, one of the most notable of which is a portrait of Catherine the Great on horseback and dressed in the uniform of the Semenovsky Guards, which hangs on the east wall of the Throne Room. This is not one of the allegories that were so characteristic of the decorative painting of the Baroque, but an historical canvas showing the Empress's return to Peterhof at the head of the Guards Regiment. The walls are also decorated with bas-reliefs of an allegorical nature by Ivan Prokofiev, namely "Truth and Virtue" and "Justice and Safety", and on historical themes, such as "The Return of Sviatoslav" by Mikhail Kozlovsky and "The Baptism of Olga" by Andrei Ivanov. At the eastern end of the room is a special platform on which the throne stands. Four pictures by Richard Paton depicting episodes from the naval battle at Chesma Bay hang on the opposite wall. Furthermore, around the edges of the room, in the spaces between the windows of the upper row, twelve oval portraits of members of the royal family are to be seen. The palace's small Chinese Studies are unique works of art in their own right. Created to designs by Vallin de La Mothe, they are decorated with genuine Chinese lacquered screens brought to Russia during the time of Peterhof's first owner. The walls of the studies are upholstered with crimson and gold silk. Against this rich background, the wooden panels painted with the miniature

349 Great Palace
Western Chinese Study

350 Great Palace
Western Chinese Study
Tiled stove

designs so characteristic of late 17th – early 18th century Chinese art are particularly striking. They show domestic scenes and landscapes as well as birds and animals, fruits and flowers. Chinese motifs were also used in the decoration of the varnished tiles with which the stoves in the respective studies are faced.

One of the oldest of the palace interiors is the Portrait Gallery. In the Petrine era this was also the largest room. The big, two-tone hall in the very centre of the palace has windows and doors on two sides. To the south the Upper Park is to be seen, while to the north lie the Grand Cascade and the gulf in all their glory. Not only does this make the already impressive room with its 7 metre high walls all the more commanding, but more importantly, it establishes a link between the interior and the natural surroundings. The room's furnishings – the painted ceiling, illustrated medallions and gilded woodwork – do not detract from its principal treasures: the walls of the gallery are entirely covered with 368 portraits by the Italian artist Pietro Rotari. This kind of "wallpapering" was characteristic of palace interiors in the 18th century. The paintings depict young men, women and girls in a variety of costumes. The uniform size of these bust-length illustrations promotes the integral impression of the many works divided by their gilded frames. This unique collection occupies a special place amongst the monuments to art of the second half of the 18th century.

351 Pyramid Fountain. 1721–1800

352 Roman Fountain. 1738–1817

The Grand Cascade divides the Lower Park into east and west, each side having its own smaller cascade. In the eastern area of the park, the Chessboard Hill or Dragon Cascade adorns a natural incline. At its head, three fantastic winged dragons spit water from between their fanged jaws, which flows down a chequered slope. Both sides of the cascade are decorated with marble statues made by early 18th century Italian masters. In front of the Chessboard Hill stand two Roman Fountains, which were created in the early 1800s. They were originally made of wood,

but were refashioned in marble at the end of the century. They resemble the two-tiered fountains on the square in front of St Peter's Cathedral in Rome. The ensemble of the Lower Park is distinguished by its unusual fountains, each of which is truly unique. Most of them are trick fountains intended for amusing visitors.

The "Pyramid Fountain" is completely different by design with its granite pedestal sat on three marble steps. This water obelisk is an impressive sight: seven tiers of foaming jets spring from over five hundred concealed apertures. Together with such monumental ornaments, the park also contains smaller, elegant fountains such as "The Sun". The sound of the latter's murmuring streams is reminiscent of an intimate conversation, while the scattered sprays of its central jet lit up by varicoloured lights give the fountain its name.

353 Eve Fountain. 1718, sculptor: Giovanni Bonazza
1726, architect: Niccolo Michetti

354 Sun Fountain. 1724, architect: Niccolo Michetti
1772–1776, architects: Yuri Velten, I. Yakovlev

355 Monplaisir Palace
1714–1723, architects: Johann
Braunstein, Jean-Baptiste Leblond,
Niccolo Michetti, sculptor Carlo
Rastrelli. Designed by Peter I

Monplaisir Garden. 1714–1739,
gardener: Leonard Garnichfeldt.
Designed by Peter I

Wheatsheaf Fountain. 1721–1723,
architect: Niccolo Michetti
Designed by Peter I

356 Monplaisir. State Hall

Peter I's favourite abode was the palace of Monplaisir (1714–1723, architects: Johann Braunstein, Jean-Baptiste Leblond, Niccolo Michetti), which is situated close to the sea and blends harmoniously with the coastal landscape. Adjoining the central part of this one-storey building crowned with a tall roof are two glass-walled galleries, which form a delightful promenade from which both the park and the sea can be viewed. The main room of this cosy little palace is the State Hall, which appears quite large due to its eight metre high ceiling. Splendid banquets and rowdy gatherings were often held here. "In Peter's day, Peterhof, or 'Peter's Court' as it was known then, teemed with life, and guests would feast here for several days at a time. The tsar's court, according to the testimonies of foreign visitors, was as splendid as almost any of its Germanic counterparts. The feasts at the court were extremely lively. It was hard to find sober and prim assemblies around the imperial tables on such occasions. There was also very little restraint at the table: at Peter Petrovich's christening, for example, a naked female dwarf appeared on the men's table from inside

a huge cake, gave a speech to the guests and made a toast, while at the ladies table a naked male dwarf did exactly the same thing. Everyone was drunk at the royal feasts regardless of whether they were male or female" (Mikhail Pyliaev). Today, the only reminder of these "assemblies" is the enormous Great Eagle Cup, which was passed to guests who were obliged, under strict surveillance and at great risk to their health, to drain it in one go.

This palace was also favoured by subsequent Russian rulers. "Here, in quiet solitude, Her Majesty (Catherine II) developed her rich abilities by reading and observing all things unusual. During the reign of Nicholas I, balls and court holidays were held repeatedly in the rooms of Monplaisir. Yet, in particular, it was here that Nicholas Pavlovich liked to take his late afternoon tea, enjoying the fine weather and the way the dome of St Isaac's and the spire of the Peter and Paul Fortress glistened in the sun" (Mikhail Pyliaev).

In the western part of the Lower Park, is the Marly ensemble whose beauty and individuality win the hearts of all visitors to Peterhof. It was named in honour of its prototype, Marly le Rois, the residence of the French king, Louis XIV. The Peterhof Marly comprises three gardens (one of which is a water garden), the Golden Hill Cascade and, of course, several fountains. At the centre of the ensemble is the Marly Palace, standing between two ponds. The modest

357 View of the Marly Palace, the semi-circular fishpond and the Garden of Venus from the Golden Hill Cascade

358 Panorama of the Lower Park around the Marly Palace

two-storey building is reflected in their mirror-like surfaces. The palace's indescribable beauty is most apparent on bright, calm days when the water of the ponds is still and the air is clear. At times like this, as if by magic, the wonderful palace materialises before the viewer as though suspended in mid-air. It seems as if the moment will pass, leaving nothing but a reflection of the building in the still waters and erasing its physical presence. Indeed, the palace has disappeared twice in the history of its existence. The Marly Palace was initially only one-storey high (1720–1723, architect: Johann Braunstein), and a second floor was added later.

359 Hermitage Pavilion. 1721–1757,
architects: Johann Braunstein, Bartolomeo Rastrelli

360 An avenue in the Lower Park

361 Hermitage Pavilion. Reception Room

362 Chessboard Hill (Dragon Cascade). 1737–1739, architects:
Mikhail Zemtsov, Ivan Blank, I. Davydov; sculptor Hans Konrad Osner

363 Chessboard Hill. Detail

In 1899, once all of its measurements had been painstakingly recorded, the building was dismantled in order for a concrete foundation to be installed. The palace was then reconstructed with incredible accuracy and the details of its original décor were recreated. During the Great Patriotic War, the building suffered acutely from the effects of shelling and was finally destroyed when a delayed action mine exploded. At the time, it seemed that the palace had been lost for good, but it was later resurrected by skilful craftsmen. Today, it stands once more surrounded by water, greenery and the open park, captivating visitors with its silent charm. Inside the palace, on the ground and first floors, which are linked by an elegant staircase decorated with openwork, are eight small rooms. On the ground floor is the Kitchen. Here, the walls and stove are covered with two-tone tiles, which are decorated with scenes of Dutch life. The main feature of the rooms, however, is a splendid collection of paintings by Dutch, Flemish and Italian masters of the 18th and 19th centuries. The view from the windows also lends the house an atmosphere all of its own.

The Marly Palace originally served as idiosyncratic lodgings for distinguished persons, but later became a museum dedicated to the memory of its first owner. Here, many of Peter the Great's personal effects are to be seen along with genuine late 17th – early 18th century artefacts.

The Hermitage Pavilion (a title derived from the French for an anchorite's hut) is situated in the part of the Lower Park that is closest to the sea. The name indicates the purpose of such buildings, which were extremely popular in France in the 18th century and later in Russia. The Peterhof Hermitage was the first in Russia. The man behind its inception was, as always, Peter I, and in 1722 the building (architect: Johann Braunstein) was erected in the Marly Garden. Its solitariness was further enhanced by a specially created moat spanned by a small bridge. Nothing was to disturb the intimate atmosphere of this house. On the first floor is the Upper Stateroom with an area of 80 square metres, where evening music recitals and intimate suppers were held. Its main feature was a special table with a system of hoists. It seated 14 people and

364 Coat of Arms Wing
Detail of the cupola

365 View of the Coat of Arms Wing
from the Neptune Fountain

366 Upper Park
Neptune Fountain. 1716–1800

was served from the Pantry on the ground floor. Special wooden pipes, through which plates could be passed, led to each setting at the table. A bell warned guests of the imminent appearance of their next dish.

In front of the south wall of the Great Palace stretches the Upper Park. This plot of 15 hectares, divided into equal parts, is a marvellous example of regular landscape gardening. The main garden is framed with borders and hedges and encompasses four trelliswork summerhouses and four arbours. The fountains, however, play the most important part in the decorations of the garden, the most magnificent of which is the "Neptune Fountain" reflecting the popular theme of the sea. The centrepiece of this three-tiered fountain is the bearded bronze figure of Neptune, the ruler of the waves. In his hands he holds a trident, the typical attribute of his power, while on his head he wears a crown. At water level, statuesque horsemen seek to restrain plunging hippocampi surrounded by dolphins, dragons and Tritons, the escorts of the god of the sea.

At the beginning of the 19th century, to the east of the Lower Park, an extensive landscaped park began to take shape, marked with its own distinctive architectural features. Of these, probably the most striking is the Cottage, built by Adam Menelaws for Nicholas I and his wife Alexandra Fedorovna, in whose honour the grounds came to be known as the Alexandria Park. English Gothic motifs with a highly romantic flavour were used to decorate the building both inside and out. Each of the rooms of the small, cosy palace boasts its own mural, which reflects the purpose of the chamber. Together with the intricate stuccowork, the paintings lend the interiors a certain elegance and charm. The house was a particular favourite of the royal family. Here, the Empress ruled the roost. Alexandra Fedorovna's tastes were readily apparent in the décor of the rooms and the arrangement of the furniture: she personally selected the objects of applied art and paintings that were used to brighten the surroundings. Through her care and attention the Cottage became a genuine family home where the Emperor was able quite simply to be a loving husband and solicitous father.

367 Alexandria Park. Cottage Palace
1826–1842, architects: Adam Menelaws,
Andrei Stackenschneider

368 Cottage Palace
Empress Alexandra Fedorovna's
Drawing Room

369 Egor Botman. ?–1891
Portrait of Nicholas I. 1849

T sarskoye Selo is associated primarily with the names of two Empresses, Elizabeth Petrovna and Catherine the Great. The initial development of the site began under Catherine I, Peter the Great's wife, who was given the land by the Emperor. However, it was only during the reign of her daughter, Elizabeth, and through the efforts of Bartolomeo Rastrelli, who believed that palaces should be created "for the common glory of Russia", that this residence could rightfully be called Tsarskoye Selo – the Tsar's Village.

In 1744, Elizabeth Petrovna commissioned Rastrelli to build "a palace with truly splendid ornaments, fit to be an abode for the ruler of a huge empire." "At first, while the palace was under construction, the ornaments gleamed, and when Empress Elizabeth arrived to view it in the company of her entire court and the foreign ministers, they were all stunned by its splendour, and each of the courtiers rushed to express his amazement" (Mikhail Pyliaev).

Besides its importance as a royal residence, Tsarskoye Selo is also linked to certain prominent Russian cultural figures and events. Even before the days of the great Alexander Pushkin who was schooled there, Tsarskoye Selo was the site of an incident that was to be of great significance in the development of national theatre. A group of actors, under the direction of the son of the Yaroslavl merchant Fedor Volkov, made its first appearance before a royal audience in the Catherine Palace. Empress Elizabeth, who had heard a great deal about the talents of the young actors, wished to witness them for herself. Delighted by what she saw, Elizabeth invited Volkov and his associates to Petersburg, and in 1756 she issued a decree on the founding of the Russian professional theatre.

Besides staterooms, drawing rooms, living quarters, Rastrelli incorporated a chapel into his designs for the palace. It became known as the Church of the Resurrection and stood in the east wing of the building. The foundations of the chapel were laid with great pomp and circumstance

370 Catherine Palace
Cupolas of the palace church

in the presence of the crown prince, Peter Fedorovich, and his wife, the future Empress Catherine II. The latter devoted much time and care to the development of the estate and "here her genius and fine taste were revealed". Tsarskoye Selo was her preferred place to stay. "Travelling to Tsarskoye with a small retinue, Catherine divided her time between affairs of state and all manner of amusements. Every day she would take a walk in the park in the company of the knights and maids of the court... Of all the country residences, Catherine's favourite was Tsarskoye Selo. From 1763 onwards, with the exception of 2–3 years, she lived in Tsarskoye Selo in spring and spent practically all summer here, leaving in the autumn when the weather grew cold. It is here that she celebrated almost every one of her birthdays, and from here that she set out on her ceremonial journey to Petersburg on 28 June 1763 after the coronation in Moscow" (Serguei Vilchkovsky).

371 View of the Catherine Palace from the park

372 Detail of the palace exterior

373 Evgueny Lanceray. 1875–1946
*Empress Elizabeth Petrovna
at Tsarskoye Selo.* 1905

374 Catherine Palace. 1752–1756,
architect: Bartolomeo Rastrelli;
sculptor: Johann Dunker

Rastrelli remodelled the main feature of the park and palace ensemble for Elizabeth Petrovna, although they are historically known as the Catherine Park and Catherine Palace respectively. The architect not only completely altered the dimensions of the latter, but also adorned them with lavish sculptural designs inside and out. The palace's external ornaments give a highly accurate impression of the creativeness and imagination of the architect, who succeeded in endowing the 300 metre long façade with a plastic expressiveness. No expense was spared on this building: approximately 100 kilos of gold alone were used in the decorations. Rastrelli perfected the regular park that had been planned earlier, stretching out to the north of the Catherine Palace, and completed the construction of a number of park pavilions. One of these was the Hermitage, intended for the Empress's amusement and solitary leisure.

Rastrelli's work as an interior designer can best be judged by the décor of the Grand Hall. This enormous room with an area of 846 square metres is permeated with a sense

of greatness and majesty. Bright and airy, it seems even larger than it actually is because of the many mirrors, the abundance of gilding and, in particular, the spectacular painted ceiling, which creates an illusion of endless space. Rastrelli wanted the room to be perceived as an integral whole, so he concealed the stoves necessary to heat this huge hall behind false windows with mirrored glass.

The famous State Staircase of marble, reconstructed in 1860 to designs by Ippolit Monighetti, is striking for the monumental character of its design.

The Picture Hall, next-door to the Amber Room, still looks the way Rastrelli first designed it. This two-tone room spans the entire width of the palace, with windows facing both east and west. It was created to house a collection of 17th – early 18th century European paintings, which was purchased abroad in 1745. Two walls of the room are completely covered with canvases, which are of historical

375 Catherine Palace. Grand Hall
Detail of the interior

376 Catherine Palace. Grand Hall. 1752–1756,
architect: Bartolomeo Rastrelli

377 Louis Tocque. 1696–1772
Portrait of Empress Elizabeth Petrovna

as well as artistic value. The interior is also decorated with tall tiled stoves embellished with painted designs. Meanwhile, the *Olympus* ceiling provides an organic complement to the lavish décor of the Picture Hall.

During Catherine II's reign, new interiors appeared in the palace, connected to the name of Charles Cameron. The use of subtly adapted forms derived from Greco-Roman décor is characteristic of the works of this outstanding master of Classicism. This is particularly apparent in the design of the Bedchamber, the largest of Paul I and Maria

Fedorovna's private rooms. Elegant alcoves and refined decorations lend the chamber a special charm. The slender faience columns entwined with garlands and arranged with a subtle sense of rhythm, the stucco frieze (sculptor: Ivan Martos) against the pale green walls, and the delicately gilded mouldings are all reminiscent of the features of the famous Pompeiian villas. Cameron especially loved to use unusual combinations of painting, gilding, decorative fabrics and items of furniture in his interiors. In the Blue Drawing Room, for example, pale blue silk with a flower

378 Catherine Palace
Bedchamber

379 Catherine Palace
Blue Drawing Room

print serves as a delightful backdrop for the austere Classical forms of the furniture and mirrors. The standard lamps made of blue glass and positioned in the corners of the room make a delightful addition to its decorative fittings. This room is the most elegant of all the interiors designed for Paul I's wife. Next-door is the Chinese Blue Drawing Room, otherwise known as the Main Study. The silks and porcelain fittings used in the décor of this chamber were brought to Russia in the mid-18th century when trade links with China began to develop. In Cameron's day, fireplaces for heating the vast rooms first appeared in the palace chambers and were constructed precisely according to his designs. Nonetheless, it was not the interiors that brought Charles Cameron the fame he deserved, but the splendid architectural edifices that he built, of which there are several in Tsarskoye Selo.

One of the main features of the palace at Tsarskoye Selo was, without a doubt, the famous Amber Room. In 1717, small amber boards and four amber panels were sent as a gift to Peter the Great by the Prussian king, Frederick I. Anyone who ever saw the Amber Room was enchanted by it. One French author once wrote that: "This room of fairly large proportions is decorated on three sides from floor to frieze with amber mosaics. The eye, unused to seeing amber in such quantities, is captivated and blinded by the wealth and warmth of the tones, which encompass every shade of yellow, from dusky topaz to bright lemon..." During the war, the amber panels were looted, and a current exhibition is comprised of the works that were saved or restored. Fortunately, the room has nowadays regained its former splendour.

380 Catherine Palace. Amber Room

381 Catherine Palace. Picture Hall

In 1728, Tsarskoye Selo became the property of Elizabeth Petrovna following an edict issued by Peter I. Before ascending to the throne, she often came here to hunt and oversee the cultivation of the orchards on the estate. It is from here that Elizabeth Petrovna departed for Moscow for the coronation on 22 February 1742, to return within a year. During the final year of her reign she lived at Tsarskoye Selo all autumn. On 8 September 1761, the Empress began to feel unwell whilst visiting the chapel and, when leaving the premises, she lost consciousness and collapsed. She only lived for three more months, dying in December at the age of 53.

In the mid-18th century, the main entrance to the palace was located on the south side of the building. A large courtyard was laid out before it, surrounded by a decorative fence with gilded details. The gateway was crowned with the Russian coat of arms.

382   Façade of the Catherine Palace seen from the ponds

Under Catherine II, the vast park with an area of 100.5 hectares became an idiosyncratic "pantheon of Russian greatness". The unique ensemble of monuments, which includes the Chesma Column and the Column of Morea, the Kagul Obelisk and the Crimean Column, commemorates the Turkish campaigns of the 1770s and 80s, the crowning glory of the Russian forces. Around the same time, buildings that constitute stylish monuments to Russian Classicism were also erected in the Catherine Park. The largest and most illustrious of these is the Cameron Gallery, named after its designer, Charles Cameron. The Gallery and the adjoining Agate Rooms, Cold Bath, Hanging Gardens and Ramp make up a harmonious "Greco-Roman rhapsody". Catherine II once described the work of Cameron in one of her letters: "Now I have got my hands on the master Cameron, a Scotsman by birth, a Jacobin by profession and a great draughtsman, who is full of knowledge of the ancients and is renowned for his book on ancient bathhouses. Here in Tsarskoye Selo we are creating a terraced garden with bathhouses below and a gallery above. It will be charming!" Indeed, this architectural composition, which comprises several buildings created to serve a variety of functions, is inspiring for its grandeur, originality and the boldness of its design.

383 Catherine Park. Terrace

384–386 Catherine Park
Decorative sculptures
17th–18th century

The Cameron Gallery, intended for meditation, promenades, social intercourse and contemplation of the splendid landscape that stretches out on all sides, plays an important part in the ensemble. The architect chose a truly appropriate spot for it on the slope of the hill leading down to the Great Pond. The ground floor of the Gallery is made of massive stone blocks. Here were the living quarters for courtiers. The bright, glass-faced hall on the first floor, surrounded on all sides by a colonnade, seems still lighter and airier in comparison to the solid ground floor. The magnificent outer staircase with its elegantly curving flight of steps is a wonderful architectural creation in its own right. The Gallery is decorated with busts of philosophers, poets, Emperors, military leaders, gods and heroes of antiquity. The only contemporary of Cameron's whose likeness is included in this series is Mikhail Lomonosov.
The two-storey building of the Agate Rooms is angled towards the sun just as Roman thermal baths were. On the lower floor are the Cold Baths for which Cameron devised a special plumbing system. The second floor is occupied by the Agate Rooms themselves, named after the material with which the walls, columns and pilasters are covered (they are also faced with jasper). The interiors of all the rooms are amazing for the harmonious combination of architecture, painting and sculpture.

387   Cameron Gallery
View of the colonnade

388   Cameron Gallery
Main Staircase

389   Cameron Gallery. 1784—1787,
architect: Charles Cameron

390   View of the Agate Rooms
from the Hanging Gardens

Tsarskoye Selo is not simply dear to Russians because it was one of the imperial country residences for many years and now constitutes a priceless architectural and artistic monument to the 18th and 19th centuries. This place is also inseparably linked to the name of the great Russian poet Alexander Pushkin, who studied at the Lyceum (now a branch of the Pushkin Museum) and continued to visit the village at various times throughout his life. Even people who have not been to Tsarskoye Selo can clearly picture its various features and get a feel for their charms when reading the poet's verses. It seems that the writer extols every inch of the park, including the renowned "Milkmaid Fountain" (1816, sculptor: Pavel Sokolov), which was built over the only natural spring in the park. Not far from the fountain is a statue depicting a youthful Pushkin in the gardens of Tsarskoye Selo (1900, sculptor: Robert Bach).

391 Cameron Ramp. 1792–1794, architect Charles Cameron

392 View of the Cameron Gallery from one of the arches of the ramp

Besides the palace and the Cameron Gallery, the Catherine Park contains a number of small pavilions, which serve various purposes. Often located on the shores of a pond or lake, they are magically reflected in the still surface of the waters. The Grotto or Morning Room (1749–1761, architect: Bartolomeo Rastrelli) blends beautifully with the panorama of the Great Pond. It is a characteristic example of the small architectural structures that adorn the horizons of the park at Tsarskoye Selo.

From the 1770s onwards, a preoccupation with "historical" styles such as the Gothic and, in particular, the Oriental "Turkic" and "Chinoiserie" styles, became apparent in the architecture within the gardens. On the shore of the Great Pond, for example, the Admiralty ensemble, consisting of three buildings, was created (1773–1777, architect: Vasily Neyelov). The name is derived from the fact that the central structure was used as a boathouse. Its round turret and the arrow slits cut into the brick walls are a testimony to the English Gothic style.

In the Catherine Park, on the southwest shore of the Great Pond, stands the Turkish Bath (1850–1852, architect: Ippolit Monighetti). Built in honour of Russia's victory over the Turks in the war of 1828–1829, its design embodies a Turkish theme.

393 Cameron Gallery
Decorative vase

394 Catherine Park. Chesma Column
1774–1776, architect: Antonio Rinaldi

395 Catherine Park. Turkish Bath
1850–1852, architect: Ippolit Monighetti

396 Catherine Park. Admiralty
("Holland"). Aviary. 1773–1777,
architect: Vasily Neyelov

*Having given his brainchild
the external appearance
of a mosque with three-tiered
minarets, the architect then
embellished the interior with
genuine articles of Eastern
applied art, namely marble
slabs taken from fountains and
carved with verses in Arabic.*

397 Catherine Park
Grotto (Morning Room). 1749–1761,
architect: Bartolomeo Rastrelli

398 Catherine Park. Palladian Bridge
1772–1774, architect: Vasily Neyelov

399 Catherine Park
Fountain: *The Milkmaid,
or the Girl with a Pitcher.*
1816, sculptor: Pavel Sokolov

The Chinoiserie style found its
embodiment at Tsarskoye Selo
in a number of bridges in the
Catherine Park and, in particular, in the ensemble known as
the Chinese Village (1782–1798,
architects: Vasily Neyelov, Charles
Cameron; 1822, architect:
Vasily Stasov). The latter
comprises 10 houses with
intricate lines and decorative
curved roofs. Situated in the
Alexander Park, this complex
is linked to the Catherine Park

400 Alexander Park. Great Caprice
1770s–1780s, architects: Vasily Neyelov,
Giacomo Quarenghi

401 Alexander Park. Cross Bridge
1776–1779, architect: Vasily Neyelov

402, 403 Alexander Park
Chinese Village. 1782–1798,
architects: Vasily Neyelov, Charles
Cameron, Antonio Rinaldi;
1817–1822, architect: Vasily Stasov

by two bridges. One of these
is the Great Caprice, which
constitutes a unique work
of park architecture. The bridge
is crowned with an elegant
pagoda in which the European
form of the octagonal rotunda is
combined with an Eastern-style
upturned roof.
The second is the Cross Bridge,
a fascinating structure
consisting of two intersecting
spans. On the bridge itself stands
an octagonal pavilion with
a curved roof, which sports
an ornamental spike topped
with a sphere.

404 Alexander Palace. 1792–1796,
architect: Giacomo Quarenghi

405 Egyptian Gate. 1827–1830,
architects: Adam Menelaws, I. Ivanov

406 Vladimir Makovsky. 1846–1920
Portrait of Nicholas II

Catherine II commissioned the building of this palace for her favourite grandson, Alexander I. She personally oversaw the education of Paul's eldest son, and patronised him in a number of ways. The Empress wanted to make him her heir in order to deprive Paul, whom she disliked, of his right to the throne and thus vex her son even after her own death.

When Alexander became Emperor after the assassination of his father, which was committed with Alexander's mute consent, the palace was given to the future tsar, Grand Duke Nicholas. Alexander III also lived there prior to his ascension to the throne, and Nicholas II chose the palace as his permanent residence. The Alexander Palace became the last refuge of the royal family after Nicholas II was deposed in 1917. From here, he and his family were taken to Tobolsk and then to Ekaterinburg, where they were executed in July 1918.

The architectural wonders of Tsarskoye Selo are not only to be seen in the grounds of the parks, but also in the town. On the road that runs alongside the Alexander Park, the Egyptian Gates, designed by Menelaws, were erected in 1827–1830.

The gateposts that flank the arch resemble truncated pyramids. They are decorated with rows of reliefs showing genuine Egyptian characters. The stylised stems of the sacred Egyptian flower, the lotus, are entwined in the metal grille. These gates formed the main entrance to the town from the Petersburg side.

407 View of the gates and main courtyard of the Catherine Palace

408 Main gates. Detail

The park and palace ensemble of Pavlovsk is situated just south of Tsarskoye Selo. In 1777, Catherine II made a gift of the extensive hunting grounds along the banks of the Slavianka River to her son Paul, and two years later work began on the construction of a formal palace and the landscaping of the natural environs. Created within a relatively short space of time (from the late 1770s to the early 1800s), it became the only country estate on the outskirts of Petersburg to have complete stylistic integrity. Within just twenty years of the laying of the first foundations, the Pavlovsk ensemble was already an inspiration to those who saw it.

In 1794, one foreign visitor to Pavlovsk made the following observations: "Pavlovsk, built in 1780 by His Highness Grand Duke Paul Petrovich, lies at a distance of 5 versts from Tsarskoye Selo in undulating countryside with small hills covered with mixed woods at the top of the Slavianka River, which flows down to the Neva. The Grand Duke's castle, set in the English Garden, is not very big but consists of three floors and two wings. The ground floor is set aside for the servants, while the top floor is for the ladies of the court. The middle floor, on which the Grand Duke resides, is arrayed with great splendour and the most exquisite taste. The location of the palace provides a wonderful view of many of the various rural features of this country. The garden is huge and laid out in the English style with hedges, meandering paths, the Slavianka, waterfalls, ponds, summerhouses, small buildings and several monuments."

The Pavlovsk architectural and park ensemble is an outstanding monument to early 19th century Russian culture. The beauty of Pavlovsk Park and the expressive designs of the palace and pavilions alike have always held a great attraction for artists. The number of paintings and sketches devoted to Pavlovsk is exceeded only by the extensive graphic records of Petersburg.

PAVLOVSK

409 Pavlovsk Palace. 1782–1786, architect: Charles Cameron; 1786–1799, architect: Vincenzo Brenna; 1800–1825, architects: Giacomo Quarenghi, Andrei Voronikhin, Carlo Rossi

The crown prince, Paul Petrovich, and his wife, Maria Fedorovna, put a great deal of effort into turning their family nest into one of Europe's most beautiful palaces. Within the walls of their residence they assembled an extensive collection of paintings, porcelain, ornamental metal-work and furniture. Under the names of Count and Countess Severny (meaning literally, Northern), the royal couple travelled around the continent familiarising themselves with the latest trends in European art and purchasing a great number of works. Paul and Maria Fedorovna's impeccable artistic tastes enabled them to identify the finest embodiments of the new Classical trends of the day. After the murder of Emperor Paul I, his widow became the sole owner of the palace and parks at Pavlovsk, and nurturing its aesthetic development became her overriding preoccupation. Sophie Dorothea of Wurtemburg, the future Maria Fedorovna, came to Russia from a small German town when she was 16 years of age. She made a significant contribution to the cultural evolution of her new homeland. Famous writers and poets of the times gathered at the salon of the widowed Empress, causing Pavlovsk to become known as the "Russian Parnassus". Maria Fedorovna compiled the first catalogue of the collections of artworks at Pavlovsk with a description of each of the objects on view there. As an enthusiastic housewife, Maria Fedorovna was also extremely keen on gardening and oversaw the development of the parks of Pavlovsk with great interest.

410 Pavlovsk Palace
Statue of Paul I. 1872
Copy from an original by Ivan Vitali

411 Panorama of Pavlovsk Palace

Two generations of Classical architects, renowned for their professional contributions to the city of Petersburg, worked at Pavlovsk. The first and most important Pavlovsk architect was Charles Cameron, whose name is primarily associated in the history of Russian architecture with the buildings he designed for this estate. The palace built for the crown prince, Paul, and his family became the dominant architectural feature at Pavlovsk. By design the palace is a threefold structure, consisting of a central section in which the staterooms and living quarters are located, and two side wings for the servants, which, together with the semicircular galleries that join them, delineate the main courtyard.

The unusually elegant gold and white façade of the central section of the palace was built to designs by Charles Cameron between 1782 and 1785. It looks particularly striking from the banks of the Slavianka, which flows at the foot of the hill on which this delightful edifice stands.

The face of the building that overlooks the courtyard continues to this day to reflect the ideas of Vincenzo Brenna, who took Cameron's place as chief architect in 1786. A statue of the first owner of the Pavlovsk Palace, Paul I (1872, from an original by Ivan Vitali), stands in the centre of the courtyard. Brenna was also responsible for designing the majority of the palace interiors. Although they

It is to Charles Cameron that the Lower or Egyptian Vestibule owes its striking appearance, so named because of the twelve Ancient Egyptian-style statues that line the walls. Above their heads medallions depicting the signs of the zodiac are to be seen, while at their feet lie the attributes of the months, symbolising man's various seasonal pursuits. These sculptures (1803–1804) were created from sketches by Andrei Voronikhin, who was invited to work on the restoration of the palace interiors after the building was damaged by fire in 1803. From the Lower Vestibule one ascends a sweeping staircase to the first floor where the Upper or Main Vestibule is located, furnished in 1789 to designs by Vincenzo Brenna. From this room a decorative wooden door, created from sketches by Giacomo Quarenghi, opens onto the Italian Hall, which lies in the centre of the palace. This is one of the most glorious of the staterooms. The interior design is the work of Cameron, who derived his inspiration from antique architecture. The hall is crowned with a high dome with skylights all round, reminiscent of a Roman rotunda. The walls of the room are punctuated with curved niches housing genuine works of Roman sculpture, themselves copies of Greek originals.
The piers of the niches are decorated with antique reliefs.

412 View of Pavlovsk Palace from one of the northern pavilions

413 Pavlovsk Palace Grecian Hall

414 Pavlovsk Palace Egyptian Vestibule

were fully furnished and fitted by 1794, the definitive image of the palace was not complete until 1825.

It is not only the wonderful architecture – one of the crowning glories of the epoch of Russian Classicism – and the splendid ornamental fittings of its interiors that have brought Pavlovsk Palace the world-wide acclaim it deserves. The valuable canvases and antique sculptures together with the magnificent array of Russian and French furniture, tapestries, bronzes, assorted clocks, ornamental vases and chandeliers to be found in the palace make it a prominent historical and artistic landmark in Russian culture. The palace's greatest treasure, however, is the furniture created by the famous French cabinet-maker Henri Jacob specifically for the State Bedroom. It is in this chamber that an extremely rare specimen of applied art is to be seen, namely, the famous Sèvres toilet set that was presented to Grand Duke Paul and his wife, Maria Fedorovna, by the French queen, Marie Antoinette, when they were visiting Paris in 1782.

The arches of the hall's upper gallery repeat the curves of the niches at ground level, creating a sensation of buoyancy and pellucidness. Light plays an important part in the aesthetic image of this particular room. During the daytime, the natural light that gently filters down from above creates an atmosphere of intimacy and mystery. At night, when the incredibly beautiful chandeliers and French horn-shaped candelabras are lit, the room becomes truly majestic and commanding. The Italian Hall was originally designed by Vincenzo Brenna, and later, after the fire of 1803, it was redeveloped by the architect Voronikhin.

In 1789, Brenna created another magnificent room in the Pavlovsk Palace, the Grecian Hall. This room too was restored by Voronikhin following the fire of 1803. The room is lined with a Corinthian colonnade, which gives it the appearance of a Greek peristyle. The Roman-style marble lamps situated between the columns are also reminiscent of antiquity. The stuccowork on the ceiling, the depictions of Roman armour and weapons on the walls and the plaster copies of antique statues in the niches lend this room a particularly lavish and august air. Voronikhin incorporated two unique white

415 Pavlovsk Palace
Third Anteroom
Clock. Late 18th century
Workshop of Pierre-Auguste Caron

416 Pavlovsk Palace
Great Throne Room
(State Dining Room)

417 Pavlovsk Palace
Great Throne Room
Girandole. Late 18th century
Imperial Porcelain Factory,
St Petersburg

marble fireplaces into the interior of the Grecian Hall, which had been made to sketches by Brenna for the Mikhailovsky Castle. The furniture of the Pavlovsk Palace was created from drawings by Voronikhin. During the era of Classicism in the early 19th century it was common for architects to design items of applied art as well as the buildings that housed them. In the southern part of the palace lies the State Bedroom (1792, architect: Vincenzo Brenna), which was no less luxurious than any of the bedchambers to be found in the royal residences of France. The walls of the room are covered with silk panels painted with tempera. They are generously laden with depictions of fruit, musical instruments and agricultural implements – symbols of "rustic joy".

The ceiling of the bedchamber is designed to resemble the trellis of a bower entwined with vines. Through the gaps in the greenery glimpses of peacocks can be seen, representing domestic happiness. The State Bedroom also contains a unique suite of furniture, the work of Henri Jacob, together with the toilette presented to Paul I and his wife by Marie Antoinette. The cobalt blue porcelain of each of the 64 items of the toilet set is decorated with delicate gold designs, while two cups bear the portraits of Marie Antoinette and Louis XVI. The palace's Picture Gallery occupies a room that forms a sweeping curve and is lined on both sides with windows,

418 Pavlovsk Palace
Italian Hall

419 Alexander Roslin. 1718–1793
*Portrait of Empress
Maria Fedorovna.* 1777

filling the room with natural light (1798, architect: Vincenzo Brenna). The pictures are hung according to a strict decorative principle. Amongst the many European paintings the most eye-catching are the works of the Flemish masters. The collection also includes canvases painted by celebrated European artists at the request of the palace's owners. The Large Vestibule or Throne Room situated in the south wing of the palace is the work of the architect Brenna. It is here that Paul I received the knights of the Order of Malta. The vast room (400 sq. m.) was originally rather low-ceilinged: the architect was reluctant to make it any larger for fear of detracting from the main suites in the central section of the palace. A brilliant master of perspective painting, Pietro Gonzago, proposed three designs for ceiling paintings that would visually increase the height of the room and create an illusion of spaciousness. It was only upon the restoration of the palace in 1957 that one of Gonzago's ideas was realised by a group of artists working under the direction of Anatoly Treskin. Today, the imperial tableware is on display in the Great Throne Room, including the famous Gold Dinner Service comprised of over 600 pieces (1828, Imperial Porcelain Factory, St Petersburg).
More modest but no less beautiful and elegant apartments are located on the ground floor of the palace. One of the finest examples of these is the Lantern Study (1807, architect: Andrei Voronikhin).

420 Pavlovsk Palace
Picture Gallery

421 Pavlovsk Palace
State Bedroom

422 Pavlovsk Palace
Lantern Study

The latter is regarded as a peerless masterpiece of early 19th century Russian interior design. The architect substituted the outer wall of the room with a semicircular oriel window overlooking the Private Garden, thereby creating a link between the palace interior and the surrounding landscape. The sunlight streaming in through the large French windows creates an enigmatic play of light and shadow. The vault of the semicircular rotunda rests on four columns, while the arc of the vault is supported by figures of caryatids (sculptor: Vasily Demut-Malinovsky).

423–426 Pavlovsk Palace. Exhibition of 19th – early 20th century interiors

The original idea and the general concept behind the layout of the main areas of the park, which now covers an area of 600 hectares, were conceived by Charles Cameron. Work began in 1782 with the laying of the main pathways leading from the palace, around which a stretch of regular park was created. Over ten pavilions were erected during the first stage of the creation of the ensemble designed by Cameron, which subsequently became the compositional centrepieces of various corners of the park. The most notable of these is the Temple of Friendship (1780–1782), the architect's first work in Russia. He built the rotunda on a small peninsula and encircled it with a ring of 16 columns. The Temple of Friendship, which presents

427   Pavlovsk Park. Centaur Bridge. 1799–1805,
architects: Charles Cameron, Andrei Voronikhin

428   Pavlovsk Park. Statue: *Apollo Musagetes.* 1798,
cast by Edmonde Gastecloux. Copy of an antique original

429 Pavlovsk Park
Apollo Colonnade. 1782–1783,
architect: Charles Cameron

430 Pavlovsk Park
Statue: *Erminia*. Mid-19th century,
sculptor: Rinaldo Rinaldi

a gorgeous sight from a variety of viewpoints, is a wonderful complement to the romantic beauty of the landscape. Cameron's last architectural contribution to Pavlovsk was the Pavilion of the Three Graces (1800–1801), a portico in the guise of an ancient temple. Its pediments are decorated with high reliefs depicting the gods Apollo and Minerva (sculptor: Ivan Prokofiev). The edifice was given its current title in 1803 when a sculptural group by Paolo Triscorni showing three female figures supporting a vase was installed inside. Cameron envisaged Pavlovsk Park as the abode of the god and patron of the arts, Apollo, and the refuge of the Muses. The architect erected the so-called Apollo Colonnade (1782–1783) almost at the entrance to the park from the Tsarskoye Selo side, a horseshoe-shaped structure somewhat akin to a Classical rotunda with a double row of sturdy columns crowned by the vault of the heavens. The material chosen for this work was grey limestone, the coarseness of which was intended to give the impression that the monument dated from a bygone era. In the centre of the colonnade stands a statue of Apollo Belvedere (1782, cast from a mould of the antique original).

After Cameron's dismissal, Vincenzo Brenna assumed responsibility for the further development of the park. In particular, he busied himself with designs for the layout

A large part in the design of the park was played by Pietro di Gottardo Gonzago, who also contributed to the palace interiors. He created entire landscaped areas that highlighted the inherent beauty of the natural surroundings themselves.

As an architect and set designer Gonzago devised a special system for planting trees and shrubs based on the different times at which they bloomed and faded to ensure that the park would be a riot of colour from early spring to late autumn, in other words the entire time that the members of the royal family would be inhabiting the summer residence.

Pavlovsk Park is characterised by the highly original and diverse artistic trends in park and garden design that prevail within its confines. The landscaped areas that expose

nature's charms, together with the many pavilions, architectural structures and sculptures have brought great repute to the Pavlovsk ensemble. The park is not only adorned with Classical monuments, however. Amidst the thickets of trees and shrubs on the banks of the river, occasional glimpses of structures of a completely different kind may be caught. In accord with the wishes of his employers, who paid tribute to the sentimental, romantic moods that were fashionable at the time, Charles Cameron built the Dairy (1782), a "theatrical" rendering of a settler's abode. It is hidden in the thick of the woods not far from the palace. Made of rough stones and thatched with straw, the outer shell of the Dairy does not betray any of the elegance and luxury hidden inside. Here, the members of the ruling elite and their guests would rest during their walks in the park and drink fresh milk from the cows that were pastured nearby. One of Vincenzo Brenna's buildings was the Peel Tower (1795– 1797) with a water mill in the spirit of the sentimental, idyllic conceits of the 18th century. It was an imitation of an old ruin adapted for living purposes by settlers. However, as with the Dairy, the cosy and beautifully finished interior was a far cry from the building's modest exterior.

431 Pavlovsk Park
Pavilion of the Three Graces
1800–1801, architect: Charles Cameron

432 Pavlovsk Park. Dairy
1782, architect: Charles Cameron

433 Pavlovsk Park. Peel Tower
1795–1797, architect: Vincenzo Brenna,
designed by Pietro Gonzago

434 Pavlovsk Park
Monumental staircase
Descent to the Slavianka valley

435 Pavlovsk Park
Temple of Friendship. 1780–1782,
architect: Charles Cameron

of two new areas, which came to be known as Old and New Sylvia respectively (from the Latin for "forest"). Old Sylvia is a quiet, secluded part of the park at the centre of which is a small circular clearing with twelve avenues leading from it. It is decorated with a bronze sculpture, the subject of which perpetuated Cameron's notion of Pavlovsk as the abode of Apollo. The sculpture of the god (1782, cast from a wax model by Fedor Gordeev) stands in the centre of the clearing surrounded by figures of the nine Muses, Venus, Flora and Mercury (1782, cast from wax models by Fedor Gordeev), which are placed between the pathways. These sculptures blend in beautifully with the landscape, lending the ensemble a special charm.

T he territory of Gatchina, which for many years previously had belonged to the principality of Novgorod, was under Swedish dominion in the 17th century. It was reclaimed from the Swedes during the Northern War, and in 1702 became a part of the Russian state. Peter I bestowed the land upon his favourite sister, Natalia Alexeevna. After her death, it became the property of various private owners. In 1765, Catherine II presented Gatchina to her famous favourite, Grigory Orlov, as a sign of her gratitude for the part he had played in placing her on the throne. That moment marked the beginning of the rich history of a magnificent country estate, which was spectacular even in Orlov's day.

Antonio Rinaldi, who had come to Russia in 1751 and become architect to the crown prince (the future Emperor Peter III), was appointed to build a palace, the foundations of which were laid on 30 May 1766. The building, reminiscent of a medieval castle, was an imposing colossus with twin square towers. Curved wings linked the main section to a pair of symmetrically placed, single-storey outbuildings, which served as the stables and the kitchen respectively.

After Orlov's death, Catherine bought Gatchina and subsequently gave it to her son Paul in 1783. "Gatchina Palace and Paul! The two are inseparable, they are so well suited and have exercised such a strong influence on one another. The strange, enigmatic Emperor, and the strange 'incomprehensible' palace. Yet most surprising of all is the fact that the palace was not intended for Paul, although it seems to have been made for him. It is hard to imagine anything other than the royal Gatchina recluse when we recall the life of Catherine the Great's heir. Paul left such a mark on the 'spirit' of the Gatchina buildings that it seems only fair to call Gatchina Paul's creation" (Nikolai Lanceray). Vincenzo Brenna, Paul's favourite architect, altered the external appearance of the palace somewhat,

436 View of Gatchina Palace from the park

368

increasing the height of the outbuildings on either side. The right-hand wing, once occupied by the stables, was converted into a storeroom, which came to house a collection of weapons and was thus referred to as the Arsenal.

In front of the palace, the existing meadow was transformed into a huge square, bordered by a moat and a stone wall. Drawbridges spanned the former, while cannons could be seen protruding from the embrasures in the wall. These were fired on public holidays and to mark the arrival of distinguished guests.

Like a true castle, the palace had its own underground passageway, which stretched northwards from the building for a distance of 120 metres. It was installed in Orlov's day, and Brenna later rebuilt and reinforced the tunnel walls.

437 Gatchina Palace. 1766–1781, architect: Antonio Rinaldi

438 Gatchina Palace. Ground Floor Gallery

Under Paul I, the palace apartments too underwent significant changes. Not only were they adapted to meet the needs of their imperial residents, but they were also decorated in fine style. The Marble Dining Room, for example, gained a new ceremonial air as a result of the magnificent fittings, central to which was the fireplace, embellished with a beautifully framed mirror. The once modest study of the master of the house became Paul I's grandiose Throne Room and, in turn, the architectural centrepiece of the palace ensemble. On the second floor, notable for its simple décor, the Emperor's sons had their suites.

After 1796, Gatchina was raised to the status of a town by order of the Emperor. A town hall, hospital, college, church and post office were built there, along with glassworks and a porcelain factory.

The magnificent Gatchina Park complex comprises three parks, the most significant of which is the Palace Park. The latter covers an area of 143 hectares, almost a third of which is occupied by lakes that are dotted with islands, which in turn are linked by bridges of various styles. One of the most striking of these is the Humpback Bridge (1800–1801, architect: Andrean Zakharov), which has become a unique symbol of Gatchina. It is quite rightly considered to be one of the most beautiful monuments to Russian Classicism. The bridge also serves as an excellent vantage point from which the wonderful surroundings can be viewed.

439 Gatchina Palace
Marble Dining Room

440 Gatchina Palace
Anteroom

441 Gatchina Palace. Empress
Maria Fedorovna's Throne Room

Beside the walls of the palace itself, on an artificially created plot of land, lies the Private Garden (1794–1797, architect: Vincenzo Brenna), one of four small, regular gardens in the western part of the Palace Park. From here, a flight of granite steps led up to Paul's personal apartments. Decorated with marble sculptures acquired by the Emperor during his travels around Italy, the garden resembled a unique open-air stateroom. Only Paul himself and his personal guests had the right to admire the scenery, hence its name.

A similar regular garden, created for the quiet leisure of select society, was laid out on the Island of Love near the northern shore of the White Lake, the largest in the park. The island's main feature is the Temple of Venus, which was an almost exact replica of the one in the grounds of Prince de Conde's estate in Italy. Although it is striking from all angles, this edifice blends in organically with its surroundings. The small Priory Park lies in a separate part of the grounds on the shore of the Black Lake. This quiet wooded area became the setting for the Priory (1798– 1799, architect: Nikolai Lvov), a symbol of "romantic" Gatchina. While in France, Paul, the grand master of the Knights of Malta, visited the priory dedicated to the order and belonging to Prince de Conde. On his return to Russia, he decided to build a similar house for himself on his country estate.

442   Private Garden. 1794–1797, architect: Andrean Zakharov

443   Gatchina Park. Humpback bridge on Long Island. 1800–1801, architect: Andrean Zakharov

444   Gatchina Park. Temple of Venus on the Island of Love. 1792–1793

445   Priory on the shore of the Black Lake. 1797–1799, architect: Nikolai Lvov

In the 1840s, the architect Roman Kuzmin transformed the modest Arsenal into a new palace. Over two hundred state and private rooms were fitted out on the first floor for the use of the families of Nicholas I and later Alexander II and Alexander III. On the ground floor, around the edges of the building, were chambers for the court attendants. A statue of Paul I, designed by Ivan Vitali, was installed in the centre of the square.

During the time that it was inhabited by the ruling elite, Gatchina Palace became renowned for its splendid, imposing and beautiful interiors, the décor of which re-

flected the changing styles of the times. It also became the home of a splendid collection of Russian and Western European paintings and objects of applied art, all of which revealed the personal tastes and predilections of the palace's owners. Alexander III was particularly fond of Gatchina and chose it as his permanent abode, prompting his contemporaries to nickname him "the hermit of Gatchina."

At present fundamental restoration work is in progress, and the vast park surrounding the palace is emerging once again as one of the most beautiful natural settings in Russia.

446 Panorama of Gatchina Park

447 Vladimir Makovsky. 1846–1920
Portrait of Empress Maria Fedorovna. 1912

T he park and palace ensemble at Oranienbaum lies to the southwest of Petersburg. Its origins are linked to the name of Peter I's friend and associate, Alexander Menshikov, who was given the land in 1710 by the Emperor himself. In 1743, Elizabeth Petrovna bestowed Oranienbaum upon her nephew and Peter the Great's grandson, the future Emperor Peter III. This "strange" figure cast a mysterious shadow over the history of Russia, and his absurd life and tragic death still arouse great interest today. He came to the throne as a result of one of Elizabeth's whims, but his coarse tastes, unwholesome habits and contempt for all things Russian and Orthodox led to his inevitable demise. Within just one year, Peter III had succeeded in turning the whole of Russian society against him. His subjects could not forgive his admiration for King Frederick II of Prussia and his betrayal of the interests of the Russian nation. Peter III's wife, Catherine, a clever and highly educated woman succeeded in exploiting these circumstances, playing on the loyal sentiments of the officers of the guards. The Orlov brothers, who lead a coup against Peter III, forced him to sign a letter of abdication on 28 June 1762. This historic event took place within the walls of the Great Palace at Oranienbaum, after which the Emperor was taken to Ropsha, where he was killed on 7 July 1762.

In the Upper Park at Oranienbaum a palace and park ensemble comprising Peter's Palace, the Honorary Gates and the Peter Park was created in honour of the crown prince, the future Emperor Peter III, and named Peterstadt.

At the same time, a palace was built which remains standing to this day. This was Antonio Rinaldi's first project in Russia. It is a simple and modest structure with the appearance of a cosy two-storey house with small rooms. A spiral staircase leads to the first floor where Peter's chambers were located. The largest and most beautiful room in the palace is the Picture Hall where the rows of canvases have a particularly striking effect. The panels, doors and wooden surrounds are covered with varnished imitation Chinese

448 Sliding Hill Pavilion
1762–1774, architect: Antonio Rinaldi

449 Great (Menshikov) Palace
1711–1727, architects: Giovanni Mario
Fontana, Johann Braunstein,
Gottfried Schaedel

450 Peterstadt. Peter III's Palace
1758–1762, architect: Antonio Rinaldi

Having been presented with a vast expanse of land on the southern shore of the Gulf of Finland by Peter I in 1710, Alexander Menshikov decided to build a residence close to the imperial estate at Peterhof and the island of Kotlin on which the Kronstadt Fortress was being built. After Peter's death, Menshikov assumed the leading role in the government of Russia. The very best architects, sculptors and carvers in the land were enlisted to work on his palace.

Amongst the palace's domestic outbuildings stood hothouses in which exotic fruits were grown, including oranges. It is possible that this is where the name Oranienbaum (German for "orange tree") hails from.

The overall design of the Great Palace, often referred to as the Menshikov Palace, was the work of Andreas Schlüter. The central two-storey section is linked by ground floor galleries to two side wings, referred to as the Church Wing and the Japanese Wing. Above the tall double-ledged roof typical of the Petrine era soars a tower, a belvedere adorned with a crown. The palace was erected on a high terrace overlooking the gulf and the outlying parks. It is in the building's indissoluble link with the surrounding landscape that its true charm lies.

To the north of the Great Palace is the Lower Garden, one of the first regular parks in Russia, decorated with sculptures, fountains, elegant flowerbeds and hedges. At one time it was intersected by a canal, which linked the palace with the gulf.

The vast Upper Park lies to the south of the Great Palace. It was developed at a time when park designers were already beginning to turn away from the "regular" style and emphasise the natural beauty of the landscape instead.

The park and palace ensembles of Oranienbaum are the unique creations of Antonio Rinaldi. The architect devoted almost twenty of his thirty years in Russia to them. Yet it is not only the carefully conceived design of the Upper Park ensembles, the originality of the architectural styles of the buildings and the artistic value of their interior décor that make it possible to speak of the exceptional nature of Oranienbaum. More importantly, the land was not seized by the Germans during the war, although the enemy lowered just outside the town for 29 months. Nor was the park and palace complex reduced to ruins. The monuments of Oranienbaum are not replicas of artworks of a bygone era, but are original in every sense of the word.

451 Peter III's Palace in Peterstadt
Picture Hall

452 Lucas Conrad Pfandzelt
Portrait of Peter III

designs in accordance with the style of the times. The walls of the remaining rooms are upholstered with coloured fabrics. The Private Villa ensemble was built on lands purchased in the early 1760s by the princess of Anhalt-Zerbst who was given the Orthodox name of Ekaterina Alexeevna and went on to become Catherine the Great. Only a few of the many buildings designed by Rinaldi and erected in this part of the Upper Park remain. Of these, "Her Highness the Empress's little house," later known as the Chinese Palace, and the Sliding Hill Pavilion are worthy of special note.

In the 18th century, *chinoiserie*, based upon Chinese motifs, became widespread in Russian decorative art. The Chinese Palace (1762–1768) is an outstanding example of this style. Moreover, it houses an exquisite collection of genuine Chinese works of art. The centrepiece of the palace interior is the large stateroom, which opens out onto further suites of rooms to the east and west. To the west, the state suites terminate in the Large Chinese Study (the Billiard Room) which boasts a highly original design. As in so many of Rinaldi's creations at Oranienbaum, the corners of the room are rounded and the walls and ceiling meet in a smooth curve.

The furnishings reflect the fantastical notion of China that was held by the people who designed and decorated them. The walls are decorated with wooden panels depicting scenes of Chinese life set against the background of a landscape. The entire composition is complemented by the illustration of *The Union of Europe and Asia* on the ceiling (mid-19th century, artists: Serafino and Giuseppe Barozzi).

To the east of the Great Hall lies the Buglework Room, which was a wonder of applied art in its heyday. The room was decorated with twelve bugled panels in gilded carved frames.

The opulence and originality of the room's fittings are further enhanced by the moulded plaster panel over the fireplace – one of the finest examples of stuccowork in the palace – and the ornamental parquet floor. In the 18th century,

453 Upper Park. Statue: *Diana the Huntress.* 18th century

454 Chinese Palace. 1762–1768, architect: Antonio Rinaldi

the floor was decorated with pieces of smalt, thus the interior was once referred to as the Mosaic Room.

The Sliding Hill Pavilion (1762–1774) is the only remaining architectural component of an enormous complex structure made up of open galleries and multiple slopes. The idea behind it sprung from the traditional Russian winter leisure pursuit of sledging down icy slopes. The elegant, three-storey, 33 metre high pavilion, situated at the top of a tall incline, is a dominant feature of the Upper Park. The building is essentially circular with three rectangles placed symmetrically around it.

455 Chinese Palace. Great Hall

456 Chinese Palace. Buglework Room

457 Chinese Palace. Large Chinese Study (Billiard Room)

458   Chinese Palace. Muse Room. Detail of a mural

459   Chinese Palace. Muse Room

Twenty nine kilometres from the mouth of the Neva, on the island of Kotlin in the Gulf of Finland, the fortress of Kronschlot was consecrated in the presence of Peter the Great on 7 May 1704. The Emperor himself chose the site of this stronghold and at one time even considered founding the capital there. Responsibility for overseeing the construction of the sea fort, which was to defend the waters of the Neva, was conferred upon Alexander Menshikov. Kronschlot saw its first military action in June 1704, and over the course of the next two centuries the sailors stationed there fulfilled the Emperor's instructions to the letter: "To defend this citadel...to the last man, whatever happens."

Besides the installation of the fortress, batteries and fortified harbours, work was started on the creation of a system of canals and the construction of docks, some of which are still in use today. At the end of the 18th century, the entire Petersburg Admiralty was transferred to Kotlin, filling up the whole of the centre of the island with its buildings and specially dug canals. In the 19th century, a great deal of time and attention was devoted to the building of new stone fortifications, which remain standing.

Under the protection of the fortress, a town began to take shape in 1714 with straight streets and canals designed to drain the marshy, low-lying land. Like Petersburg, the town was developed according to a specific plan. In contrast to the nearby metropolis, however, this small town, christened Kronstadt in 1723, has borne the same name to this day. From the very beginning, Kronstadt was envisaged not only as a habitation for sailors and soldiers, but also as a major port, which was supposed to play an important part in local trade. The commercial port remained on Kronstadt until 1885, after which it was relocated to Gutuevsky Island in Petersburg.

Kronstadt is also the home of a monument to the founder of the Russian fleet and the very fortress itself, Peter I (1841, cast by Piotr Klodt). The life-size figure of the

460 Anchor Square
Naval Cathedral. 1903–1913,
architect: Vasily Kosiakov,
artist and architect: N. Podberezsky

Monument to Admiral Stepan Makarov
1913, sculptor: Leonid Sherwood

Kronstadt is a city of maritime glory, and all of its most interesting edifices and monuments reflect this theme. Amongst the religious architecture, the most significant building is undoubtedly the Naval Cathedral (1903–1913, architect: Vasily Kosiakov) on Anchor Square, the historic centre of the city. The square was named in 1754 when a warehouse for storing anchors and chains taken from defunct vessels was erected upon it. The cathedral at Kronstadt was intended to serve as a memorial to "members of the Naval Department who died in the performance of their duties." The cathedral is an impressive example of the late "Byzantine" style. St Sophia's Cathedral (6th century AD) in Constantinople served as its prototype. The Naval Cathedral is essentially a square, elongated to the east and west by two semicircles. It stands at a height of 70.62 metres, and the large cupola is 26.7 metres in diameter. The outer walls are faced with granite and brick, decorated with terracotta ornaments and majolica friezes. Slabs of black marble engraved with the names of the dead adorn the inner walls.

In the same year that the cathedral was consecrated, a monument was erected on the southern side of Anchor Square in honour of the brilliant naval commander, academic and polar explorer, Rear Admiral Stepan Makarov, who died during the Russo-Japanese War. The statue is the work of the sculptor Leonid Sherwood.

461 Warships in Petrovskaya Harbour

Emperor, dressed in the naval uniform of his day, holds his head up high and rests his right hand on the hilt of a sword. The monument stands on a pedestal, the corners of which are embellished with stylised acanthus leaves in the popular style of the 18th century. On the front of the pedestal an inscription reads: "To Peter the Great, founder of Kronstadt, 1841", while on the opposite side the words of the Emperor's decree of 1720 are carved: "The protection of the fleet and the defence of this place to the last are paramount."

Until recently, Kronstadt was strictly out of bounds for tourists. Today, however, it is linked to the mainland by a road that runs along the tidal barrier, and anyone who wishes may visit the island in order to enjoy the beauty and originality of both the naval fortress and the town.

462 On duty

463 Anchors and chains around the monument to Stepan Makarov

464 Monument to Emperor Peter I. 1841, sculptor: T. Jaques, cast by Piotr Klodt

465, 466 The embankment of Obvodny Canal

467   A glimpse of Kronstadt

САНКТ-ПЕТЕРБУРГ

Альбом (на английском языке)

Издательство «П-2»
191119, Санкт-Петербург, Звенигородская ул., д. 11
Тел./факс: +7 (812) 320-92-01, 320-92-11 E-mail: info@p-2.ru
Отпечатано в ОАО «Иван Федоров» (7814)